"To think laz … punching bag for our s… … Usually, Christian thinking about gender starts with your church's tradition or a few Bible verses ripped from their context. This is what makes the ideas presented in *Biblical Femininity* so refreshing. It starts with God himself, and then thoughtfully and practically surveys the biblical data offering a fresh paradigm for understanding his design. I have used portions of this material in premarital counseling, marriage seminars, and even in systematic theology classes! If you want to think well about biblical femininity, you have to read this book."

— Jim Thompson, equipping pastor at Fellowship Greenville and author of *A King & A Kingdom*

"This book offers a relevant and refreshing voice to the often-dreaded subject of biblical femininity. Written with grace and thoughtfulness, it draws all women to embrace their lifetime calling through the truth of the Word and the freedom of the gospel. This challenging reflection speaks to the very nature of our soul and what we were created to be—strong and supportive women who reflect the very image and glory of God."

—Cheri Jimenez, pastor's wife, Taylors First Baptist Church and former speaker for Council on Biblical Manhood and Womanhood

"*Biblical Femininity* offers a refreshing look at what it means to be a woman—and thankfully that definition doesn't have anything to do with whether or not we are married, have children, or bake our own bread. It has everything to do with our identity and calling, neither of which is defined by roles. This book will open your eyes to the freedom that comes when we embrace who we really are as women created in the image of God."

—Ruthie Delk, author of *Craving Grace* and women's conference speaker

BIBLICAL *FEMININITY*

Discovering Clarity and Freedom in God's Design for Women

GRACE CHURCH

Biblical Femininity: Discovering Clarity and Freedom in God's Design for Women

ISBN: 9798857878835
Library of Congress Control Number: 2023915637

Design and illustrations by Madei Click

CONTENTS

ACKNOWLEDGEMENTS

The creation of this book is a story involving years of dedication, development, and contribution by Grace Church leaders and members. It would be impossible for this book to exist without the direction and persistence of Bill White, the hours of study and research contributed by Ryan Donell, and the wisdom, biblical knowledge, and direction of Virginia Griffin. Thank you.

Thank you to Julia Taylor, who led the original curriculum team as editor and provided the framework for much of what exists now, and to Jim Taylor for his theological insight. Thank you to Heather Nelson for the wisdom and insight you contributed to the original curriculum team and for making sure this book remained rooted in the gospel.

Thank you to Mark and Renee DeMoss for opening your home for an entire weekend so that the curriculum team could have quiet space to think and create. Thank you to Joy Jones for embodying the *ezer* calling, for serving the curriculum team, and for championing the women's ministry of Grace Church with your hours of dedication. Thank you to Renee DeMoss, Keri Geary, and Abby Moore for the time and energy spent editing and re-editing, making this a polished, accessible product.

To our faithful test readers: Alicia Matthews, Jenny Talbott, Bailey Edmonds, Debra Williams, Allyison Merritt, Barbara Dansby, Chris Curtis, Christa Moormeier, Cindy and Mike Chibbaro, Cristin Henry, Joy Jones, Emily McGowan, Emily Voelkert, Jim Taylor, Libby Thomas, Maria Weaver, Leah Pinckney, Lee Anne Cavin, Molly Burns, Rachael White, Taylor Beard, Trina Thiry, and Ruthie Delk. Thank you for your vital insight, feedback, and sensitivity!

Thank you to the Ambassador International team—Brenda Covert, Tim Lowry, Anna Raats, and Hannah Nichols—who have labored alongside us through the publishing process. We are grateful for your commitment, diligence, and dedication to the *Ezer* resources.

And finally, thank you to all of the women at Grace Church who have filled out surveys, attended development meetings, provided feedback, led our studies, and ultimately championed our cause. This study is the fruit of your contributions, and we are forever grateful for the time, energy, and resources you have invested.

PREFACE

After more than eight years of dialogue, argument, and research, I have come to the following conclusion: gender is a big deal. Our distinctiveness, as male and female, lies at the heart of what it means to mirror the image of God in the world. The categories established in Genesis 1 through 3 still dominated the Apostle Paul's thinking thousands of years later, and he did not hesitate to apply them with startling clarity to the church of his day. I would argue that we must undertake the same work in our generation.

This book is the product of one church's struggle to understand the implications and applications of what the Bible says about femininity. We are a church filled with people from every conceivable religious and irreligious background, but we are swimming in the waters of fading Southern fundamentalism. We live in a conservative context and serve a group of women who carry wounds from an obsessive pursuit of clarity and control. But even in the Bible Belt, we increasingly engage an emerging generation of young women who are obsessed with self-expression and view gender as just another way to express their individuality. The consequences of this quest for absolute freedom are terrifying beyond imagining.

What you hold in your hands is the product of what Marva Dawn would call "Spirit-led consensus." No one person can claim to be the author of this work; rather, it is the product of a local community seeking to do God's work and understand his way. I am certain that we still have much to learn, but I do believe we have something to say that might be of help to other churches who are striving to help women reclaim the glory of femininity as a reflection of the image of God. May God make it so.

—Bill White
Teaching Pastor, Grace Church

01

AN ESSENTIAL COUNTERPART

> So God created man in his own image, in the image of God he created him; male and female he created them.
>
> —Genesis 1:27 (ESV)

IMPOSSIBLE STANDARDS

What does it mean to be a woman or a man? What is it that makes you masculine or feminine? Posing this question to a group of young people today is always an interesting experiment. Silence often fills the room, and perplexed looks wash over their faces. No one is quick to speak, but eventually someone musters up enough courage to speak, and then eventually others follow suit. Their answers often include things like physical makeup, mental and emotional processes, and how you relate to people.

But are these accurate metrics by which you can define what it means to be masculine or feminine? If masculinity and femininity are defined by how you relate to people, what does it mean when a man is more relational than a woman? The same is true with mental and emotional processes. If a man is more sensitive and emotionally charged, does this mean he is not masculine? What if a woman is more analytical and good with numbers but is relationally awkward?

This uncertainty and lack of clarity leaves many unknowingly struggling to find solid ground upon which they can base their identity. Our need for clarity drives us to create rules and standards for ourselves so we can know we measure up. Then we apply those same standards to all women. Women who work outside the home look in judgment on women who stay at home with their children, believing that they are wasting their potential. Women who stay at home with their children look in judgment on those who work outside the home, believing they are abdicating their role as a wife and mom. Married women look in pity on single women, believing they are somehow incomplete without a spouse and children. Mothers who homeschool their children look in judgment on those who place their children in the public school systems, and mothers who place their children in public school systems look in judgment on those who homeschool their children.

This confusion has caused much pain and turmoil for women trying to navigate through today's world. One woman stated:

> "Within these stereotypes of womanhood, there are impossible standards for success, making some girls feel like they will never become the woman they're supposed to be. While they try to sort through the confusion, girls see wealthy but isolated businesswomen, proud but unfulfilled housewives, and exhausted women who struggle to fill both roles at once. On the other side of the spectrum, "successful" women still receive criticism. Our culture seems to label motivated women in the workforce as too aggressive, especially in male-dominated fields, and dedicated mothers as too submissive or even apathetic in their life goals. It's no wonder girls head into womanhood looking like a deer in the headlights."[1]

As a result of all of the confusion and stereotypes, many young women fight against their own femininity, seeing it as weaker, subservient, and less valued than their male counterparts. They strive to be free of any perceived constraints, and model their leadership, their ambitions, and their thinking after men. Others create their identities around a distorted version of femininity, reducing it to roles like wife and mother, and base it around legalistic ideals that marginalize, even patronize, femininity. This type of thinking tends to create rules such as women should not work outside of the home or hold positions of leadership. So they strive to conform in an effort to measure up and follow the rules. But both of these views lack the power and glory of true biblical femininity as God created it and as displayed through the Scriptures. One strives for absolute freedom, which leads only to the tyranny of self and makes you a slave to your own desires. The other strives for absolute clarity and control, so you don't have to trust God, and leads you to self-righteousness. And in the end, all this produces is embittered, frustrated, exhausted women who somehow feel they can never quite measure up.

Questions for Reflection

1. What do you think it means to be feminine?

2. Based on that definition, do you feel like you measure up, or do you miss the mark? Why?

A CULTURAL SNAPSHOT

There is, no doubt, much confusion surrounding gender in today's world, in both secular and traditional religious cultures. Some now argue that while one may be born with a sex, gender is a choice. What began as a fight for gender equality in the feminist movement is now transitioning into a fight for gender neutrality.

Freedom and individual rights are highly valued in today's culture—so much so that any truth not self-defined is often viewed as restrictive, oppressive, and unjust. This worldview is a form of relativism—a belief that there is no real truth except that which is defined by the individual. The results of this movement are landmark changes occurring around the world. In early 2012, Sweden introduced the word hen as a new gender-neutral pronoun, replacing the traditional he or she.[2] Also ushered in during 2012 is the inclusion of the first transgendered Miss Universe contestant.[3] Both of these examples illustrate mankind's attempt at defining oneself—the quest for identity outside of social, cultural, and religious norms.

While the modern feminist movement may not be leading the charge toward gender neutrality, the rallying cry is still one of self-determinism. It is a fight against absolutes, standards, or constraints. It is a belief that women can be and do, should be and do, anything they want. It is a fight not just for equality, but also for sameness in which gender distinctions are eradicated.

There is no doubt that the feminist movement has been a catalyst providing women with great opportunities such as the right to vote, the right to work, the Family and Medical Leave Act, and equal opportunity for jobs, salary, and benefits. Women, who once had to fight for these rights, now outnumber men in colleges and in the workforce.[4]

Yes, we are witnessing the rise of women. But at what cost? Women are twice as likely to suffer from depression and anxiety as men. Approximately seven million women in the United States alone suffer from clinical depression.[5] *Could it be that in seeking freedom, women have actually found a new form of bondage?*

On the other end of the continuum is the extreme traditionalism of some religious cultures. This view of femininity often gravitates toward a strict code of ideals and a role-based mentality centered on that of wife and mother. This results in a belief that adhering to moral standards shapes a woman's identity and earns her approval as a woman. Religion is mankind's attempt to adhere to moral standards, not godly standards. These standards, whether real or perceived, often prove burdensome and discouraging to women who do not fit this mold.

Based on these traditional standards, singles and women without children often feel they are incomplete apart from a man or children. Likewise, women with gregarious personalities or those who work outside of the home often feel like they too somehow miss the mark when it comes to living out biblical womanhood. Women find it difficult to live up to these standards because they are founded on false ideals.

Like feminism, traditionalism has a positive contribution to make as well. While they are not exclusive to traditionalism, morals, belief in biblical truth, and family values may well find roots from more traditional ancestors. *But, while seeking to adhere to biblical truth and standards, could it be that traditionalists have created a standard of femininity that is too narrow?*

Ironically, while these opposing views look very distinct on the outside, they are both ways to attain autonomy—an individual status or identity, apart from God. Both are so deeply entrenched within culture that women will likely find themselves on one end of the continuum or the other.

While there are positives to both views, both are equally destructive. Neither end of the continuum accurately portrays the magnificence of the image of God as displayed through femininity. So what is the answer? There is a third way of thinking that is not on the continuum between these two mistaken opposites. In an article called "The Centrality of the Gospel," author and pastor Timothy Keller describes this third way dynamic:

> "Since Paul uses a metaphor of being 'in line' with the gospel, we can consider that gospel renewal occurs when we keep from walking 'off-line' either to the right or to the left. The key for thinking out the implications of the gospel is to consider the gospel a 'third' way between two mistaken opposites. However, before we start we must realize that the gospel is not a halfway compromise between the two poles—it does not produce 'something in the middle' but something different from both. The gospel critiques both religion and irreligion (Matthew 21:31; 22:10)."[6]

The goal is not to find the perfect halfway point between these two incorrect views but to find freedom from them. This freedom can be found only in the power of the gospel.

Questions for Reflection

1. Toward what end of the feminism/traditionalism continuum do you lean? Are you seeking absolute freedom to define yourself as you wish? Or are you caught on the performance treadmill, trying to control and measure up to what others think you should be?

2. In what ways might you be experiencing bondage to your current views of femininity?

3. How is your view of femininity different from that of other generations, such as your daughter, mother, or grandmother? What are the strengths and weaknesses of their views? What are the strengths and weaknesses of your view?

GOAL OF THIS STUDY

The Bible reveals that God created mankind in his own image—as male and female (Genesis 1:27). This means that God is the one who created the distinctiveness of maleness and femaleness. Gender is not a false construct of society, but straight from the mind of God who chose to create male and female to reflect his image in distinct ways that bring him glory. However, this too is subject to sin and the brokenness brought about by sin, and as a result we have witnessed the destructiveness of religious oppression as well as cultural self-expression. But this need not lead us to eradicate gender altogether. Rather, like all of God's good creation, it must be redeemed.

Someone once said that if you want to change a culture, you need a theology and a common language. We have seen this to be true. If we, as Christians, are going to generate helpful discussion around the chaos and confusion surrounding gender and the difference between personality, roles, and design, then we must speak the same language. If your job sends you to work in a foreign country where you do not speak the language and your coworkers do not speak your language, you will not be able to accomplish much together. However, if you speak the same language, you will be able to make great strides toward accomplishing your goal. The same is true of discipleship. This study is meant to be a discipleship tool for women. While it may be good to read alone, it is better when these truths are discussed and worked out within the context of biblical community. Our goal is to provide a practical, helpful resource that equips women to think biblically about what it means to be a woman and that provides a common language with which women can speak in order to spur one another on toward growth in spiritual maturity.

This study aims to be a clear and distinct biblical voice amid the confusion by providing a theology and language for what it means to be a female image-bearer. We believe that a basic understanding of femininity should be derived from Scripture—Scripture that is still culturally relevant today. We do not desire to create a caricature of femininity or an artificial cultural box, thereby depriving women of the power and glory of the image of God as it expresses itself through godly femininity. Defined standards, such as those that require Christian women to work in the workplace, homeschool their children, or dress a certain way, marginalize women and limit the diverse ways in which God has designed women to reflect his image and glory. On the contrary, our goal is to provide women with CLARITY and FREEDOM. We strive to be as clear as the Scriptures and to provide women with freedom from rigid constructs so that they might be free to reflect and glorify God in their own distinctiveness.

WHAT IS *EZER*?

> Then the Lord God said, "It is not good for the man to be alone. I will make a helper who is just right for him." . . . So the Lord God caused the man to fall into a deep sleep. While the man slept, the Lord God took out one of the man's ribs and closed up the opening. Then the Lord God made a woman from the rib, and he brought her to the man.
>
> —Genesis 2:18, 21–22

The *Ezer* study is derived from the Bible's story of creation found in the first two chapters of the book of Genesis, which will be explored in more depth in the following chapter. These beginning chapters of the Bible reveal that humanity was created in the image of God: male and female—equal, but different. Each gender uniquely represents the glory of God. This is too significant to simply skim over. Men and women were created by God, in the image of God, and for the glory of God. And as the Creator, he alone gets to determine their identities.

More specifically, as it pertains to feminine creation, God says, "I will make a helper who is just right for him," or as some translations say a "helper fit" or a "helper suitable." In the original Hebrew, this is *ezer kenegdo*. However, when these words are translated into their English equivalent, they lose the robust Hebrew meaning. Through the years, the word helper has taken on a negative connotation. It seems weak, patronizing—not substantial enough. *Ezer* means one who helps, one who brings that which is lacking to the aid of another. An *ezer* assists another toward accomplishing a goal. Thus the word *ezer* actually connotes an inherent strength. The word *kenegdo* means corresponding to. So joined together, *ezer kenegdo* means essential counterpart or corresponding strength.

A good illustration of this can be drawn from a 12th century architectural innovation called the flying buttress. Commonly used in Gothic architecture, the flying buttress provides essential support that preserves the architectural soundness and integrity of a building. These buttresses bear the weight and relieve pressure from the walls, allowing for higher ceilings, ornate latticing, and more windows. Like these powerful structures, a woman provides an undergirding strength within the context of relationship that empowers another to become and achieve things that might have otherwise been impossible. She is an essential counterpart providing necessary, load-bearing support.

The word *ezer* is used twenty-one times in the Old Testament, the majority of which refer to God. *Ezer* is used twice in the Genesis creation narrative, specifically pertaining to women. Throughout the rest of Scripture, it is used three times as a military term, and sixteen times

God identifies himself as an *ezer* (see Psalm 146, 54, 70, 118). *Ezer* is not a weak word; it is a strong word. An *ezer* is someone who is for you, an ally—someone who supports, aids, rallies to your cause, and brings you strength. And God entrusted his *ezer* nature to women so that they might reflect his character in this distinct and powerful way.

Given an understanding of the Hebrew and seeing *ezer* in other contexts, one can appreciate the significance of the *ezer* calling. As *ezer kenegdo,* femininity is a strong and necessary part of the combined reflection of God. The feminine reflection was not the inferior, second thought of an absent-minded Creator. It is the beautiful, intentional completion of the divine portrait. A woman's core calling is to be an *ezer.* Women primarily mirror the *ezer* nature of God. For the remainder of the study, we will shorten *ezer kenegdo* to *ezer.*

Everything about what it means to be a woman is essential and valuable. Women reflect God in and of themselves. That's important. As a woman, your value is not first in what you do, but in who God created you to be, who you are as his reflection.

Another vital thought is that a woman's nature is one that corresponds. One of the things this means is that a woman's identity is irreducibly tied to relationship. In the context of marriage, one can see the necessity of both male and female image bearing. Femininity is uniquely suited to find and meet need in the context of relationship. Although Scripture introduces the design of woman in the context of marriage, a woman can still gain understanding of her unique image bearing regardless of marital status.

In the book, *God's Good Design,* author and theologian Claire Smith states:

> "Man's problem in the garden was not singleness; it was solitude. He was alone, not unmarried. Sexual differentiation means none of us is alone—as Adam was alone—because we are all in relationships—more than that, we are all in gendered relationships. All of us relate to men and women, as parents, siblings, friends, workmates, at church—in fact,

> everywhere we go. And, so with varying degrees of intimacy, all of us experience the complementarity, the dance, between women and men."[7]

Female image bearing is fully adequate beyond the bounds of marriage. That is to say, healthy and robust femininity does not depend on marriage for its expression, but it is expressed fully within the context of community and interpersonal relationships.

This raises an important distinction. There is often confusion between role and identity, between function and design. We are not talking about roles, but about identity. Women tend to define themselves by roles (student, career woman, boss, mother, wife, grandmother, etc.) or by the absence of such roles. But there is danger in defining yourself by a role you play. Roles are often temporary, lasting for a season. Some roles, like that of wife or mother, may span decades. Other roles such as student, employee, athlete, or single are shorter, lasting just a few years. Roles may bring clarity to how and with whom you live out your calling, but they do not determine your identity or your calling.

Your **identity** is certain and secure; it does not shift. You are a human being created in the image of God. You were created as a woman. Your calling is an outflow of your identity as a created being. As a woman created in the image of God, your calling is to be an *ezer.*

Ezer is not a role; it is a lifelong calling. It is part of your DNA, so to speak. *Ezer* is not limited to one role; it is who you are. It is a God-given design. Women are not defined functionally by roles; they are defined inherently by how God created them. Like your identity, your calling as an essential counterpart, *ezer kenegdo,* never changes.

Questions for Reflection

1. Read Psalm 146. List the ways in which the Lord is an *ezer*.

2. How does understanding God as our *ezer* change how you view your calling as an *ezer*?

PERSPECTIVES OF BIBLICAL FEMININITY

Every woman was created to reflect the *ezer* nature of God. But how a woman lives out her calling, as an essential counterpart, looks different because every woman is different. This is where theologian John Frame's work on viewing truth through multiple perspectives may be helpful. Frame believes that by considering three perspectives—knowledge of God's norm (the unchanging truth of God's Word), knowledge of our specific situation, and knowledge of ourselves—we can better understand and apply truth to our lives. By bringing these three perspectives together, we begin to gain clarity into what it means to reflect the *ezer* nature of God (the norm) in distinctive ways as individuals, in a variety of seasons and circumstances.

The triangle illustration below identifies the three perspectives of biblical femininity: Calling (knowledge of God's unchanging truth), Season (knowledge of your specific situation), and Individuality (knowledge of yourself). As you seek to apply your calling, it is important to consider these three perspectives. The illustration is a helpful tool to provide clarity on how your calling as an *ezer* plays out in your life.

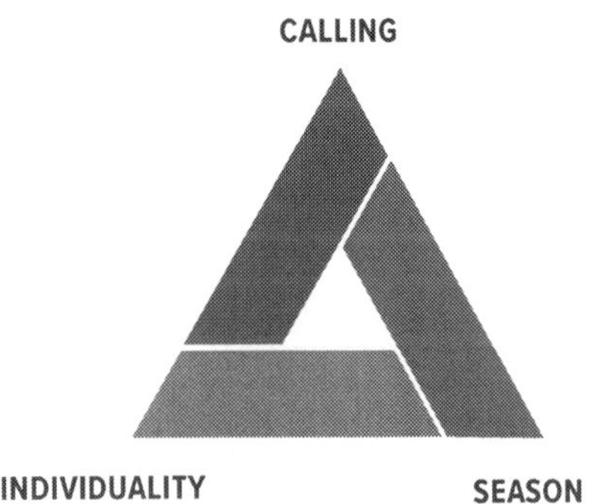

CALLING – At the top of the triangle is your calling. A calling is the purpose for which you were created. You were created, as a woman, to reflect the *ezer* nature of God. This is your calling, and it is common to all women. Being an *ezer* is primary, and it is the only unchanging component of femininity. It is who you are and who you were created to be. There is great CLARITY in this area based on the truths of Scripture.

SEASON – At the bottom right of the triangle is your season. "Season" is a way of referring to roles, age, circumstances, or relationships at a specific time. Seasons change and, as they do, they may bring new roles, circumstances, priorities, and needs. A woman could be single, a wife, an employee, a supervisor, a mother, or a student at any given point in time.

INDIVIDUALITY – "Individuality" is what makes you you. Your individuality includes your gifts, passions, interests, personality, backgrounds, sins, wounds, strengths, weaknesses, etc. Individuality, like season, also changes as you age and mature. God takes the good and bad of your individuality and weaves it together to equip you as an *ezer*. There is great freedom in this area. Knowing that God uses your uniqueness, you are freed from trying to model yourself after any other woman.

What does all this mean, and why does it matter? As a woman, your calling is certain. You were created to be an *ezer*, to be one who comes alongside as a corresponding strength or essential counterpart. This is who you are, and that never changes. But how you live out your calling, and with whom, is clarified through your individuality and season of life. For example, a woman with a strong shepherding gift, in a season of helping her aging parents, may not have the time or energy to mentor a young teen. The same woman, in a different season of her life, may be able to spend considerable amounts of time and energy in a discipleship relationship. Her individuality (her shepherding gift) and her season (helping aging parents) factor enormously in how she lives out her calling on a daily basis.

There is clarity about our common calling as women, but there are many legitimate expressions of this calling. The individuality displayed in Scripture is vast and encouraging, bringing freedom from rigid constructs and stereotypes. Throughout the Old and New Testaments, Scripture represents a diverse group of women. Anna was a widowed prophetess who served in the temple for most of her life (Luke 2:36–38). Lydia was a businesswoman, a merchant who sold her wares in the marketplace (Acts 16:14). Deborah was a judge and a prophetess (Judges 4:4). Mary, the mother of Jesus, was a young bride and mother (Matthew 1:18). Rachel was a shepherdess (Genesis 29:9), as well as a wife and mother. And Priscilla was a wife and tentmaker by trade (Acts 18:3). The point is that there is much more freedom and diversity in Scripture than we are willing to embrace.

As you seek clarity on what it means to think biblically regarding what it means to be a woman, you must consider the purpose for which God created you (to be an essential counterpart) and who you are uniquely (your individuality) as you seek to live out your calling as a woman created in the image of God in your current season or circumstance.

Questions for Reflection

1. In what ways have you felt like you do not fit society's or religion's depiction of femininity?

2. In what ways have you confused identity, role, and calling? What are some consequences you have experienced as a result of your confusion?

3. How does an understanding of the perspectives of femininity (calling, individuality, and season) change your idea of what it means to be a woman?

CORE CAPACITIES

INVITING, NURTURING, PARTNERING

All human beings have the image of God instilled within them, regardless of whether or not they are Christians. Men are uniquely designed to reflect the image of God in distinctly masculine ways. Likewise, women have the capacity to reflect the image of God in distinctly feminine ways. This idea, though biblical, has been corrupted throughout the years and, as such, the true meaning of what it means to reflect God as a man or as a woman has been distorted or in some cases lost altogether.

Masculinity is not about machismo, hunting, playing football, or blowing things up. Similarly, femininity is not about cooking, shopping, and emotional sensitivity. These false constructs lie at the root of many of culture's arguments against the perceived oppression of gender distinctiveness, and rightly so. These ideas are rooted more in a person's individuality—their own likes and dislikes, personality, gifts and talents, strengths and weaknesses—and are not necessarily gender-specific.

There are many men who are highly relational, tenderhearted, love theater, and enjoy cooking, while there are many women who are more introverted, love sports, hate to shop, and are not sentimental, hopeless romantics. The point is that reflecting the image of God as a woman or as a man is much more broad than these narrow ideas allow. So, for the purpose of this study, we will explore how the *ezer* calling is lived out through three core capacities: **inviting**, **nurturing**, and **partnering**. A *capacity* is simply the instilled ability to reflect an attribute of God. We will explore through scriptural examples how these capacities reflect the *ezer* nature of God and how he has entrusted women with these capacities to reflect him and to bring him glory.

Inviting, nurturing, and partnering are part of the constitution of every woman, but each woman brings her own individual application. These capacities can be honoring to the Lord, as intended, or corrupted through sin. Because every woman is unique, these capacities will manifest themselves in different ways, according to each woman's personality, strengths and weaknesses, and temptations and propensity toward sin.

The distinctions in genders, as they work together and complement one another, give a more complete reflection of God. Both are necessary and essential if we are to understand more about God's character. But, the image of God as portrayed through masculinity and femininity is much more robust than we are able to do justice within the pages of this study. However, as common language, these terms are helpful in encompassing much of the *ezer* calling. Throughout the remainder of the study, we will explore each of these capacities, how they have been corrupted, and how the gospel redeems them within femininity.

WHAT ABOUT SIN?

We cannot go much further without acknowledging that because of sin, the image of God as displayed through humanity, is fractured. Like Eve, all women have chosen their own way. They have chosen autonomy. And in choosing autonomy, fellowship with God and humanity was broken. Not having power to right yourself, you were destined for destruction on both an eternal level and on a daily level. You are truly powerless to change on your own.

> Once you were dead because of your disobedience and your many sins. You used to live in sin, just like the rest of the world, obeying the devil—the commander of the powers in the unseen world. He is the spirit at work in the hearts of those who refuse to obey God. All of us used to live that way, following the passionate desires and inclinations of our sinful nature. By our very nature we were subject to God's anger, just like everyone else.
>
> —Ephesians 2:1–3

The good news is that God freely gives his daughters a renewed identity. The Bible teaches that Jesus was the complete human being. He bore the image of God perfectly and in every way. Christ came to right what humanity wronged. When you trust in the gospel, you are free to live out your calling as an essential counterpart. Christ took your punishment for your sin, and in turn gave you his "perfect image-bearer" status. He offers the freedom that comes with being declared "not guilty" for all the wrongs you've committed against your Creator and gives you a new life with new potential.

> The Son radiates God's own glory and expresses the very character of God, and he sustains everything by the mighty power of his command. When he had cleansed us from our sins, he sat down in the place of honor at the right hand of the majestic God in heaven.
>
> —Hebrews 1:3

> Since we believe that Christ died for all, we also believe that we have all died to our old life. He died for everyone so that those who receive his new life will no longer live for themselves. Instead, they will live for Christ, who died and was raised for them. So we have stopped evaluating others from a human point of view. At one time we thought of Christ merely from a human point of view. How differently we know him now! This means that anyone who belongs to Christ has become a new person. The old life is gone; a new life has begun!
>
> —2 Corinthians 5:14b–17

When you begin to approach your life as a woman from this new identity, this freely given status in Jesus, you find that there are a host of arenas where this renewed femininity can be expressed. The reality is that God has chosen for his renewal to be an ongoing process. If you believe in Jesus, then you have already and completely been "approved" with his status. Nothing you do or don't do will ever add or take away from this fact. However, the work that's been done in you and for you now has to be worked out through you.

But here is where we wish to offer a word of warning. Believers tend to gravitate toward one of two poles (or somewhere in the middle). On one end is "checklist spirituality," and on the other end is "passive spirituality." The former tends toward "doing," and the latter tends toward abdicating personal responsibility.

A woman who leans toward checklist spirituality may be tempted to reduce this study to a list of to-do items to check off at the end of the day. This is a works-based mentality in which she is attempting to earn God's favor and the favor of others based on how she fulfilled her calling as an *ezer*. The danger in this type of spirituality is that she may modify her behavior, but she may never experience transformation at a heart level.

A woman with this tendency lives in an emotional and spiritual state of flux, experiencing wide swings based on her performance. When she performs well, she swings toward pride, and when she performs poorly, she swings toward despair. She is not living in the hope and freedom of the gospel but is bound instead as a slave to her own ability to live out her calling.

The Apostle Paul reminded the Galatians, who had abandoned the gospel of grace and had once again become slaves to the law, that if "keeping the law could make us right with God, then there was no need for Christ to die" (Galatians 2:21b). The good news of the gospel is that Christ's righteousness has been given to you. You can't earn it. It is because of Christ that you stand holy and blameless before God. A woman who knows and understands this is free from slavery to pride and despair. She knows her identity and acceptance rest safely in the hands of Christ, and her obedience is from a place of freedom rather than fear.

On the opposite end of the spectrum is the woman who leans toward passive spirituality. She may be tempted to inaction as she rests on God's gift of grace. For this woman, the study is just good information that she never feels the need to apply. She bases her inactivity on the fact that Jesus did it all, grace covers her, and now she just gets to live in that freedom.

She may or may not see grace as a license to sin, but she does not feel responsible to work hard to show the results of her salvation, obeying God with deep reverence and fear (Philippians 2:12).

This mentality is just as much a distortion of the gospel as is works-based righteousness. Paul exhorted the Philippians to "live as citizens of heaven, conducting yourselves in a manner worthy of the Good News about Christ" (Philippians 1:27a). The good news of the gospel is that because of Christ's life, death, and resurrection on your behalf, you have been set free from sin. You are no longer a slave to sin; but now "you must give yourselves to be slaves to righteous living so that you will become holy" (Romans 6:19b).

The heart of a woman who has been captured by the gospel will seek to live in a way worthy of the gospel. She knows and understands that she cannot earn her salvation or righteousness, but it is from that free gift she seeks to live an obedient and holy life. A woman who knows what the gift cost the Giver will live a life of obedience that flows from her grateful heart.

These things may sound contradictory, but we assure you they are not. This is the good news of the gospel: you cannot earn your salvation. Christ's blood, shed on your behalf, purchased it for you. Now you are no longer a slave to sin and death, but have been adopted into the family of God. And, having been adopted, you were given the power of the Holy Spirit to live lives worthy of the kingdom of God (Ephesians 2:8–9, Romans 6:6–7, Romans 8:15).

With that said, it is important for you to do two things: First, identify your tendency toward either end of the spectrum in order to receive the full impact of this curriculum. Second, identify what gospel solution you need, even if it is different from that to which you are accustomed. This will be hard work, but our goal is heart change, not mere behavior modification.

A WORD OF ENCOURAGEMENT

God created you to be who you are and, in Jesus, it is very good (Ephesians 2:10). There is no template for the perfect woman. Diversity is not only inherent but also necessary in the church. Jesus Christ frees you from the need to compare yourself to others. You already have an identity in Jesus. When you are living out your identity in Christ, reflected through your *ezer* calling, you can be you and glorify God. This is true freedom.

Questions for Reflection

1. Toward which type of spirituality do you lean, checklist spirituality or passive spirituality?

2. What gospel solution do you need in order to be freed from these two inaccurate views of the gospel?

3. What concerns or fears do you have about this study and how it might affect you?

4. How open are you to this study?

02

BACK TO THE BEGINNING

> In the beginning, God created the heavens and the earth. The earth was without form and void, and darkness was over the face of the deep. And the Spirit of God was hovering over the face of the waters.
>
> —Genesis 1:1–2 (ESV)

In the beginning, God . . . This is a profound and fundamental idea at the root of the Christian faith. God alone is the uncreated, self-existent one. Everything that exists in heaven and on earth exists only because God created it; all being flows from him. And as the Creator, he alone has the right to determine the identity, purpose, and boundaries of his creation:

> He is the God who made the world and everything in it. Since he is Lord of heaven and earth, he doesn't live in manmade temples, and human hands can't serve his needs—for he has no needs. He himself gives life and breath to everything, and he satisfies every need. From one man he created all the nations throughout the whole earth. He decided beforehand when they should rise and fall, and he determined their boundaries.
>
> —Acts 17:24–26

Creatures do not rule over their Creator; the Creator rules over the created. Men and women are created beings. Everything about who you are flows from this defining attribute. Every man, every woman, every living thing is subject to the One who created it. This is true of you if you are a Christian or not. As such, the relationship you have with God, as your Creator, is one of dependence for life, breath, and everything. You are fearfully and wonderfully made. God knit you together in your mother's womb—weaving you together in the depths of the earth. And every day of your life was ordained before one of them came to be (Psalm 139:13–16).

As a created being, there is much to be learned about yourself through the lens of your Creator, and who could provide you with better understanding about your purpose, your design, and your identity than the Creator himself? But the thought that you are a created being may be new to you and cause you to bristle. You may even be tempted to reject this idea and assert your own right to choose who you are and how you live. How you view God and what you believe about him will affect how you relate to him as your Creator. If you believe him to be holy and righteous but not loving, you may feel afraid to trust yourself to his rule. If you view him as loving but not just, you may view him as your wish granter more than a holy, righteous judge. But, if you view him as both holy and loving, both just and merciful, then you will approach him, as your Creator, with reverent fear and humility, as well as with trust and gratitude.

All of creation, including humanity, was made to glorify God. More specifically, within creation, mankind was appointed the privilege of image bearing. Our charge, as his image-bearers, is to multiply (produce more "reflectors" of his image) and care for (govern, order, and nourish) the rest of God's creation as his representatives. All of creation brings God glory, but mankind was created with the express purpose of revealing God in a way unlike anything else.

Questions for Reflection

1. What is your view of God?

2. In what way does your personal understanding of God affect how you currently live?

3. How might a right understanding of God as Creator and you as a creature change the way you think about femininity and personal freedom?

THE FIRST IMAGE-BEARERS

In the beginning, nothing existed but God, and yet, we see in Genesis 1:26b, when God says, "Let us make man in *our* image, after *our* likeness" (emphasis mine), that he is obviously not alone. Scripture from Genesis to Revelation reveals that God exists in eternal, perfect community within himself. God is three in one: the Father, the Son, and the Holy Spirit, which is commonly referred to as the Trinity. The relationship between the Father, Son, and Holy Spirit is one of perfect, intimate fellowship—knowing, being known, and being loved, each by the other.

Each member of the Trinity is living, vital, and active. Each played an essential role, working in harmony with one another toward the creation of the universe (Genesis 1:2b, Colossians 1:16–17, John 1:1–4). The Trinity represents unity in diversity. Each member is equal in value, yet distinct.

This same unity and diversity is mirrored in creation itself. From the very beginning, God creates and then separates. He divides light from dark, sky from sea, heavens from earth, land from water, night from day, and land dwellers from water dwellers. Each creation is significant. There is diversity and separation, but there is also unity and harmony as each creation complements its counterpart. Every created thing has a purpose assigned to it (Genesis 1:3–19).

Then in Genesis 1:26–27, we get a first look into the creation of mankind:

> Then God said, "Let us make man in our image, after our likeness. And let them have dominion over the fish of the sea and over the birds of the heavens and over the livestock and over all the earth and over every creeping thing that creeps on the earth." So God created man in his own image, in the image of God he created him; male and female he created them.
>
> —Genesis 1:26–27 (ESV)

Created in the image of God, male and female. The diversity displayed in the creation of light from dark, heavens from earth, and land from sea, is also seen in the creation of mankind. Each part of creation is distinct, yet complements its counterpart. In the creation of mankind, God yet again distinguishes them by creating male and female. They are equal in value as image-bearers, yet different in form and function as male and female. They are, like the rest of creation, complementary counterparts.

God created human beings in the divine image so they might represent him over the rest of creation. They were created for a purpose—to represent God and to be a blessing to the world.

While Genesis 1 gave us the macro view of the creation account, Genesis 2 gives us a micro view, providing us with more detail surrounding God's rationale for the creation of man and woman:

> When no bush of the field was yet in the land and no small plant of the field had yet sprung up—for the Lord God had not caused it to rain on the land, and there was no man to work the ground, and a mist was going up from the land and was watering the whole face of the ground—then the Lord God formed the man of dust from the ground and breathed into his nostrils the breath of life, and the man became a living creature. And the Lord God planted a garden in Eden, in the east, and there he put the man whom he had formed.
>
> —Genesis 2:5–8 (ESV)

The earth had been created, but it was not yet fruitful because there was no man to cultivate the ground. Creation was incomplete; the earth needed someone or something to tend it and make it fruitful. So God created man out of the dust of the earth to meet the need of the earth. Then,

> The Lord God took the man and put him in the Garden of Eden to work it and keep it. And the Lord God commanded the man, saying, "You may surely eat of every tree of the garden, but of the tree of the knowledge of good and evil you shall not eat, for in the day that you eat of it you shall surely die."
>
> —Genesis 2:15–17 (ESV)

The earth had a need. So God created the man and gave him a job to do—to work and watch over the garden. He also gave the man direction and boundaries: *You are free to eat of every tree in the garden, except the tree of the knowledge of good and evil. If you eat of this tree, you will die.*

So Adam began to work, but something was missing. Creation was still incomplete, and God declared that it was not good for the man to be alone. The Lord looked upon Adam and saw his need, declaring that there was no helper fit for him (Genesis 2:18). So the Lord's work continued:

> Now out of the ground the Lord God had formed every beast of the field and every bird of the heavens and brought them to the man to see what he would call them. And whatever the man called every living creature, that was its name. The man gave names to all livestock and to the birds of the heavens and to every beast of the field. But for Adam there was not found a helper fit for him. So the Lord God caused a deep sleep to fall upon the man, and while he slept took one of his ribs and closed up its place with flesh. And the rib that the Lord God had taken from the man he made into a woman and brought her to the man.
>
> —Genesis 2:19-22 (ESV)

God placed Adam in the garden, and he began to work, naming the animals, categorizing the creation, and establishing order over it. But as he did so, he felt his lack; there was no counterpart, no complement for him. Adam was alone. So the Lord determined to make a counterpart for Adam, one to come alongside him.

So God caused Adam to fall into a deep sleep, and he fashioned a woman out of the man. Just as Adam was created from the earth to meet a need of the earth, Eve was created from Adam to meet a need of Adam. Adam corresponds to the earth—he was placed in the garden to work it, and he was given instruction regarding it. Eve corresponds to Adam—to be his complementary counterpart, the one who would work alongside him and aid him in the mission of filling and subduing the earth (Genesis 1:28).

And Adam rejoiced over God's creation:

> Then the man said, "This at last is bone of my bones and flesh of my flesh; she shall be called Woman, because she was taken out of Man." Therefore a man shall leave his father and his mother and hold fast to his wife, and they shall become one flesh. And the man and his wife were both naked and were not ashamed.
>
> —Genesis 2:23-25 (ESV)

Adam had felt his lack, but when God brought the woman to him, he cried out, "At last!" He finally had someone like him, one to whom he could relate. And the man and woman were naked and unashamed, enjoying the abundance of creation and unhindered fellowship with God and with one another. There was no relational barrier between them as husband and wife, nor was there a barrier between them and God. They were bare before one another and before God—in perfect, intimate fellowship. There was no hiding, no shame, no fear of being known. They were fully known and fully loved, and it was good.

Adam and Eve were free. All of creation was at their disposal. Nothing was forbidden to them. Nothing—except the tree of the knowledge of good and evil. God had given Adam very specific instructions regarding this tree back in Genesis 2. And all was good in the garden, until the serpent slithered onto the scene in Genesis 3. Then everything changed.

God had created Adam, placed him in the garden to work and govern it, and gave him very specific instructions. All of this occurred before Eve was even a twinkle in Adam's eye. But the serpent turned the tables on God's created order, circumventing Adam and addressing Eve instead.

> Now the serpent was more crafty than any other beast of the field that the Lord God had made. He said to the woman, "Did God actually say, 'You shall not eat of any tree in the garden'?" And the woman said to the serpent, "We may eat of the fruit of the trees in the garden, but God said, 'You shall not eat of the fruit of the tree that is in the midst of the garden, neither shall you touch it, lest you die.'" But the serpent said to the woman, "You will not surely die. For God knows that when you eat of it your eyes will be opened, and you will be like God, knowing good and evil."
>
> —Genesis 3:1–5 (ESV)

The serpent's sole tactic was to bring into question what God had said, to insinuate that God was withholding something good from them, and to cast doubt upon God's character. He launched his attack and it was effective.

> So when the woman saw that the tree was good for food, and that it was a delight to the eyes, and that the tree was to be desired to make one wise, she took of its fruit and ate, and she also gave some to her husband who was with her, and he ate.
>
> —Genesis 3:6 (ESV)

Eve saw that the tree was good for food, delightful to the eyes, and good for wisdom, and she chose to step outside of God's direction and provision and rely on herself instead. Rather than acknowledging God's right to rule and establish boundaries over all of creation, including her, she established herself as the supreme authority and chose her own way. Eve was autonomous. But where was Adam when all of this was occurring?

He was *with* her. God had given Adam explicit instructions regarding the tree; therefore, he was ultimately responsible. Adam was supposed to step into this situation to provide direction and take responsibility, but he didn't. He didn't add his voice, his body, or his energy to the situation. Instead, he stood by passively and allowed the situation to unfold.

> Then the eyes of both were opened, and they knew that they were naked. And they sewed fig leaves together and made themselves loincloths. And they heard the sound of the Lord God walking in the garden in the cool of the day, and the man and his wife hid themselves from the presence of the Lord God among the trees of the garden.
>
> —Genesis 3:7–8 (ESV)

The result of Eve's autonomy and Adam's passivity was disastrous. Their eyes opened, revealing their nakedness, and they were ashamed. Their freedom gave way to bondage. They were exposed—both physically in their nakedness and spiritually in their sin and rebellion. Their once unhindered fellowship with God and with each other was broken. And in that moment, they attempted to cover themselves and hide in an effort to manage their problem on their own.

> But the Lord God called to the man and said to him, "Where are you?" And he said, "I heard the sound of you in the garden, and I was afraid, because I was naked, and I hid myself." He said, "Who told you that you were naked? Have you eaten of the tree of which I commanded you not to eat?" The man said, "The woman whom you gave to be with me, she gave me fruit of the tree, and I ate."
>
> —Genesis 3:9–12 (ESV)

Where Satan reversed God's created order by approaching Eve, God re-affirmed his created order by going first to Adam. As God walked in the garden in the cool of the day, he called to Adam, who was hiding and afraid. The Lord called Adam to account for this behavior, asking him if he had eaten of the forbidden tree. Again, rather than taking responsibility, Adam was passive, blaming both the woman *and* God who gave him the woman.

So God then turns to the woman.

> Then the Lord God said to the woman, "What is this that you have done?" The woman said, "The serpent deceived me, and I ate."
>
> —Genesis 3:13 (ESV)

Eve wanted responsibility; she wanted the freedom to make her own choice and to be her own god. But when God plays by her rules and calls her to be responsible for the choice she made, she too shifts the blame and throws off responsibility by blaming the serpent.

Through Eve's autonomy and Adam's passivity, sin and brokenness entered the world. And in the closing scene of Genesis 3, God pronounces the curses, starting with the serpent.

> The Lord God said to the serpent,
>
> "Because you have done this, cursed are you above all livestock and above all beasts of the field; on your belly you shall go, and dust you shall eat all the days of your life. I will put enmity between you and the woman, and between your offspring and her offspring; he shall bruise your head, and you shall bruise his heel."
>
> —Genesis 3:14–15 (ESV)

The serpent circumvented God's created order, going straight to the woman. So it is fitting that it would be through the offspring of a woman that the head of the serpent would eventually be crushed. This is the first glimpse we are given into God's promised redemption and the Savior who would be born of a woman and reverse the curse, securing full and final victory over sin and death once and for all.

Then, to the woman he said,

> "I will surely multiply your pain in childbearing; in pain you shall bring forth children. Your desire shall be for your husband, and he shall rule over you."
>
> —Genesis 3:16 (ESV)

Eve, who was created as an essential counterpart to bring strength in the context of relationship, would from now on experience the curse through those same relationships. Though she was created with a unique capacity to nurture life and bring it to full form through childbearing, it will cause her great pain to do so. And just as Eve was created out of Adam to meet a need of Adam, she would bear out the curse in the marital relationship as well. Rather than coming alongside her husband as his ally, as his complement and counterpart, now her *desire* will be for her husband, but he will rule over her. This same word for desire is used just one chapter later as the Lord warns Cain that sin crouches at the door and its desire is for him (Genesis 4:7). The idea is that she will desire to control and dominate her husband and rather than lovingly leading her and protecting her, his leadership will be harsh and oppressive.

And finally, turning to Adam he said,

> "Because you have listened to the voice of your wife and have eaten of the tree of which I commanded you, 'You shall not eat of it,' cursed is the ground because of you; in pain you shall eat of it all the days of your life; thorns and thistles it shall bring forth for you; and you shall eat the plants of the field. By the sweat of your face you shall eat bread, till you return to the ground, for out of it you were taken; for you are dust, and to dust you shall return."
>
> —Genesis 3:17–19 (ESV)

The earth, from which Adam was taken and to which he corresponds, would be cursed and produce thorns and thistles, and Adam would labor and sweat over it. The curses God prescribes to them correspond to their callings.

Questions for Reflection

1. Adam was tempted toward inaction. Rather than taking responsibility and moving into the situation in the garden, he stood by passively and let the scene unfold. How have you seen the sin of passivity play out in the lives of men in your life (father, husband, son, friends)?

2. Eve was tempted to take charge of the world around her—she knew God's instructions but instead of listening to her husband and obeying God, she looked at the tree and saw that it was desirable. She reached out and took control. How have you seen this desire for control play out in the lives of women you know (mother, sister, daughter, friends)? How are you experiencing this desire to take control in your own life?

3. It is often said that art imitates life. How are men and women generally characterized in media? How do you see the temptations toward passivity and autonomy portrayed in movies and television shows?

WHAT DOES THIS HAVE TO DO WITH US?

Genesis chapters 1–3 are foundational in our understanding about God, mankind, and sin. Each of these chapters provides detail about God's intended design and purpose for the man and the woman, as well as their core sin.

Adam was created and was given direction and responsibility to lead, but he demonstrated passivity instead. Though Adam was with Eve when she took the fruit and ate it, he was detached and disengaged. He stood by, watching and waiting to see what would happen. He did not accept responsibility for her or for God's creation. He did not stop the serpent. He did not provide direction or protection for his wife. And he did not protect the creation God had entrusted to his care. Instead, Adam was passive. Like Adam, God created men to be responsible and to lead; this is their core calling. But also like Adam, all men have the same core temptation—to be passive and not take responsibility.

Eve was created after Adam to be his counterpart, to come alongside him and bring strength. But she chose autonomy (self-rule), establishing herself to be the final authority. Eve asserted herself above God and Adam, rather than coming alongside or coming under the authority and direction of her husband. Rather than bringing her God-given strength through the relationship, she brought it over the relationship. Rather than bringing her strength and power to bear for good, she brought harm. She abused the good gift she had been given, using it for her own means instead of using it for the glory of God.

Women are powerful and influential. This is not a corruption of femininity. On the contrary, it is a good, God-given gift. But God intends women to use this unique feminine power for the good of others, coming alongside others as allies and partners, bringing strength and life in and through their relationships. This is a woman's core calling and God's perfect design. But like Eve, all women have the same core temptation—to be autonomous, reject authority, and seek control of the world around them.

When men and women live out their core calling, their relationship displays the glory, unity, and diversity of the Trinity. However, when they act on their core temptations, the result is a destructive dance. Because his core temptation is passivity, a man instinctively takes a step back in difficult situations, and because a woman was created to meet need, she instinctively takes a step forward in those situations. A man, feeling threatened by that, will take another step back. This cycle repeats as he continues to step back and she continues to step forward until he has stepped back so far that he is out of the picture altogether.

The consequences of this dance are disastrous. The man, in his passivity, is not leading and accepting responsibility given to him by God. The woman, in her autonomy, has stepped outside of her calling to be an essential counterpart, and has placed herself in a position of responsibility that was not hers to bear. In this way, she is now accountable to God and stands in a place of judgment that was intended for Adam.

This vicious sin cycle will continue until the man rejects his passivity and steps into the situation, or the woman rejects her autonomy and steps back, providing the man an opportunity to step up. It is a perfect storm. But this is not just the story of the first man and woman; this is our story, our calling, our struggle.

While we have explained how this struggle plays out between a man and a woman, we want to be clear that these core temptations are not exclusive to opposite sex relationships. Men can be passive in situations involving other men. Likewise, women can be autonomous in situations involving other women. These challenges are common and will be played out in a variety of situations, circumstances, and relationships.

Up to this point, because we are looking at the first man and woman, we have largely discussed women only in relation to men. While marriage between a man and woman is a distinct, even primary, application of gender, it is important to note that this is not about marriage. Biblical masculinity and femininity are not dependent upon marriage. If masculinity and femininity are dependent upon marriage, then half of the world's population is not fully male or female! This is about who God created men and women to be and how both reflect his image in uniquely masculine and feminine ways.

As a woman, your calling is fulfilled through your relationship with others. Women who are more introverted in nature may feel frustrated by this statement, but that need not be the case. A woman's calling is not a personality trait or a skill she must develop; it is who she is *designed* to be. Being an *ezer* is not about being outgoing, the life of the party, or having a million friends. On the contrary, how you live out your calling to come alongside others will be worked out through your own unique personality, whether introverted or extroverted. As a woman, you have a unique kind of strength that is brought to bear in the context of relationship. Women are gifted to look at a relationship, see what is lacking, and bring strength to fill in the gaps.

This does not mean that men are not relational or that women should not work, lead, or take responsibility. To make broad generalizations like that would create a false construct and marginalize both men and women. There are many men who are gifted communicators, highly relational, and compassionate nurturers. Similarly, there are many women who are gifted, powerful, and effective leaders in political and private sectors, in their communities, and in their churches. Biblical masculinity and femininity is not about personality or roles but about distinct attributes of God's character that he has entrusted to men and women as his image-bearers.

The following table displays the core calling and core temptations of men and women and the ways in which these callings are lived out (core capacities). The words we have used (invite, nurture, partner and pursue, provide, protect) are not used specifically in Scripture. However, we do believe that the concepts are scriptural. It is evident in Genesis 1 and 2 that God created Eve to be a *counterpart*, a partner to Adam. When Scripture speaks of God as a *nurturer*, the language used is often feminine (Isaiah 49:15). The book of Proverbs is a brilliant contrast of two women who display redeemed and corrupted *invitation*.

	MAN	WOMAN
CORE CALLING	LEADERSHIP/ RESPONSIBILITY	ESSENTIAL COUNTERPART
CORE TEMPTATION	PASSIVITY	AUTONOMY (Self-Protection/Self-Promotion)
CORE CAPACITIES	PURSUE, PROVIDE, PROTECT	INVITE, NURTURE, PARTNER

These capacities are not exhaustive. The image of God, as displayed through men and women, is far more robust than we are able to do justice within the pages of this book. However, while we recognize that no language is perfect, we do hope that the language used for these capacities will provide common ground upon which to meet one another and engage in fruitful dialogue about being men and women created in the image of God. We will explore these capacities more in the following chapters.

MASCULINITY*

1. **Leadership/Responsibility** - Leadership is not about personality. It is an expression of responsibility and movement. Leadership for a man is not optional; it is his responsibility and calling. How a man expresses leadership will look different based on his personality, but every man has the role and responsibility to function as a leader—finding a way to accept responsibility. It is okay if a wife is more gifted in leadership than a man is; it is about responsibility. A man is supposed to work, initiate, be an agent of reconciliation, and move into difficult situations.

2. **Passivity** - Passivity is also not about personality. It is not about being shy, being verbal or not verbal, or being compliant. These are personality traits. Passivity is the core struggle of all men. Personality will only dictate how a man manifests his passivity. Even domineering men are passive, rejecting responsibility for those entrusted to them. Men are tempted toward silence, toward stillness, toward a lack of movement, and toward abandonment.

FEMININITY

1. **Ezer/Essential Counterpart** - The core calling for a woman is to be an *ezer*. This is also not about personality. How a woman expresses her core calling will be based on her own individuality, her own unique personality. A woman is to invite others into relationship with her, to come alongside them and bring strength, and to help further their causes. The focus is on cre-

*For further study on the core callings and capacities of masculinity, see our Men's Roundtable study, *Authentic Manhood* located at grace.sc.

ating independence and strength in another that helps them become more of who God intended them to be.

2. **Autonomy** - Autonomy is self-rule, rejection of authority; it is seeing oneself as sovereign and as morally independent. The fundamental idea of autonomy directly opposes a woman's core calling as an *ezer*. However, autonomy is not the same as independence. Independence connotes strength. Left unbridled, strength can become dangerous, but strength under the restraint of God-ordained authority is beneficial. As a woman rejects her calling as an essential counterpart and embraces autonomy, she becomes further absorbed with self, resulting in either self-promotion or self-protection.[8] She will move either into a position of self-protection, defending herself from anything perceived as negative, or she will self-promote, elevating herself and leveraging her power over others.

There are many applications of self-protection and self-promotion, and the outworking of these will be as varied as the individual. A woman who is self-protective may be rigid, unapproachable, intimidating, brash, or abrasive. Or, she may be timid, withdrawn, shy, and quiet. A woman who is self-promoting may be boastful, demand attention, and dominate conversations. Or she may promote herself subtly through manipulation, pride, self-righteousness. Either extreme, or any combination of them, are corruptions of the image of God as displayed through femininity.

Questions for Reflection

1. How does the knowledge that you were created in the image of God, bearing and reflecting his attributes, change how you understand yourself as a woman?

2. Understanding that your calling as a woman is fulfilled through relationships with others, what relational challenges do you face (shy, introverted, fearful of being hurt, etc.) that affect your living out your calling?

3. In Genesis 3, we can see that the man's core struggle is passivity and the woman's core struggle is autonomy. What are some areas in which you see the sin of autonomy in your own life?

4. What does autonomy look like for a single woman? How might she place authority in her life to guard against the sin of autonomy?

3

INVITING

Genesis chapter 2 revealed that God created woman as an *ezer*, to be one who comes alongside as a corresponding strength. The *ezer* calling occurs through relationship with others, which is possible only if you engage or *invite* others into relationship with you. Therefore, for a woman to fulfill her calling as an *ezer*, she must begin with invitation.

Inviting is welcoming others into relationship with you. The capacity of inviting is active and intentional, but it is also a disposition. To *invite* someone into relationship requires action on your part. It requires extending yourself and holding yourself out to another. To be inviting describes the way in which you hold yourself out to them. Both are equally important. In order to fully explain the capacity of inviting, we must explore it as both a verb and an adjective—as both an action and as a disposition, as a state of being.

THE ACTION OF INVITING

All throughout Scripture, God reveals himself as an inviting God. He holds himself out to his people—inviting them into his presence, into covenant, into relationship. And God has graciously instilled this attribute of his character within women, who are to reflect him to the world. In order to understand the capacity of inviting within women, we must first look to Scripture to see how God invites. Isaiah 55 paints a beautiful portrait of God's invitation to humanity:

> Is anyone thirsty?
>
> Come and drink—even if you have no money!
>
> Come, take your choice of wine or milk—it's all free!
>
> Why spend your money on food that does not give you strength? Why pay for food that does you no good?
>
> Listen to me, and you will eat what is good. You will enjoy the finest food.
>
> Come to me with your ears wide open. Listen, and you will find life.
>
> —Isaiah 55:1–3a

In this passage, the Creator God invites his people to come to him to receive the nourishment they need. The invitation is broad and inclusive, extending to people without resources and without expectation of return. Time and again in the Old Testament, God invites the Israelites to come, to return to him, and to look to him for strength and life.

God extends that same invitation to all of humanity. He invites us into relationship with him. He welcomes us to himself as a source of life and strength. God's desire to invite far exceeds our desire to accept invitation or to live in community. This is why the Psalms invite over and over again. As Psalm 34:8 says, "Taste and see that the Lord is good! Oh, the joys of those who take refuge in him!"

The divine attribute of invitation comes to full light in Jesus. He is magnificent. The very features of God, in his fullness, are on display in Jesus. Through his life, death, and resurrection on our behalf, we are drawn in to know and to be known. He extends a love and a strength that has to be experienced. Jesus is the perfect image-bearer. So, it's not surprising to see him extending invitation like God the Father.

> Then Jesus said, "Come to me, all of you who are weary and carry heavy burdens, and I will give you rest. Take my yoke upon you. Let me teach you, because I am humble and gentle

> at heart, and you will find rest for your souls. For my yoke is easy to bear, and the burden I give you is light."
>
> —Matthew 11:28–30

Like the Father, Jesus extends invitation to those who are in need. He invites people to himself. Jesus lends his strength, carrying the load. Humble, meek, and gentle, Jesus offers safety and rest.

The book of Proverbs introduces two women who also invite others to come and partake, Lady Wisdom and Lady Folly:

> Wisdom has built her house; she has carved its seven columns. She has prepared a great banquet, mixed the wines, and set the table. She has sent her servants to invite everyone to come. She calls out from the heights overlooking the city. "Come in with me," she urges the simple. To those who lack good judgment, she says, "Come, eat my food, and drink the wine I have mixed. Leave your simple ways behind, and begin to live; learn to use good judgment . . ." Wisdom will multiply your days and add years to your life.
>
> —Proverbs 9:1–6, 11

Similar to God's invitation to those with no resources and Jesus' invitation to the weak and burdened, Lady Wisdom's invitation extends to everyone. She urges the simple to join her. Her invitation is sacrificial. She does not limit it based on what others have to offer her. On the contrary, she invites others based on what she can provide them. She holds herself out to them freely, openly, and without shame. She invites them to partake of what she has to offer so that they may become better.

> The woman named Folly is brash. She is ignorant and doesn't know it. She sits in her doorway on the heights overlooking the city. She calls out to men going by who are minding their own business. "Come in with me," she urges the simple. To those who lack good judgment, she says, "Stolen water

> is refreshing; food eaten in secret tastes the best!" But little do they know that the dead are there. Her guests are in the depths of the grave.
>
> —Proverbs 9:13–18

Lady Folly also calls the simple to join her. But unlike Lady Wisdom, Lady Folly is brash and ignorant. Her invitation to others costs her nothing. She has nothing to offer except that which she has stolen from someone else. She lives and thrives off others. She is a consumer rather than a provider. She is not free to live openly or without shame. Rather than inviting others to partake so that they may become better, her offer leads to their destruction.

Both women invite. Lady Wisdom displays a redeemed invitation that reflects the heart of God. However, Lady Folly displays a corrupted form of invitation that reflects the heart of sinful humanity.

Holding yourself out to another, offering your life to them, is important. But what you invite them to is equally important. Eve invited Adam—but her invitation (to partake of the fruit) led them to shame, death, and fractured relationships with God and with each other. Likewise, Lady Folly invites, and her invitation also leads to foolishness and death. Yet when Jesus invites, he invites you to himself—which leads to life, peace, and wholeness. With that said, let's take a look at the essence of inviting.

Questions for Reflection

1. In what other ways is God inviting to humanity?

2. How have you seen women invite in ways that are helpful to others? How have you seen women invite in harmful ways?

THE DISPOSITION OF INVITING

INVITING DELIGHT

God also extends an invitation to his people through creation. He created a world in which humanity was welcomed. The garden he formed invited work and rest, exploration and worship. God invited humanity into relationship with himself through a functional and beautiful environment.

Sally Lloyd-Jones writes of God's inviting work in her *Jesus Storybook Bible* as she recounts the *Story and the Song*:

> "The heavens are singing about how great God is. And the skies are shouting it out, "See what God has made!" Day after day, night after night, they're speaking to us. God wrote, "I love you." He wrote it in the sky, on the earth, and under the sea. He wrote his message everywhere. Because God created everything in his world to reflect him like a mirror, to show us what he's like, to help us know him—to make our hearts sing. The way a kitten chases a tail; the way red poppies grow wild; the way a dolphin swims. And God put it into words too and wrote it in a book called the Bible."[9]

Lloyd-Jones puts it so simply, yet so profoundly. God extends invitation to know him through his creation, and it is glorious. But when we come to the nature of femininity, we find that God's writing is not just in the sky, on the earth, and under the sea, but all the way down to the female soul.

It is true that God delights in his people (Zephaniah 3:17), but he also holds himself out to be a source of delight for his people (Psalm 37:4). He longs for us to delight in him. As John Piper says, "God is most glorified in us, when we are most satisfied in him."[10] A woman, as an image-bearer, reflects this desire of God to express beauty, promote delight, rest, and refuge. In Proverbs 5, a father urges his son:

> Let your wife be a fountain of blessing for you. Rejoice in the wife of your youth. She is a loving deer, a graceful doe. Let her breasts satisfy you always. May you always be captivated by her love.
>
> —Proverbs 5:18–19

A man is to rejoice in the wife of his youth. He is to enjoy her, to delight in her. She is to be his source of delight. Throughout the Song of Solomon, the young man delights in his bride, and she delights in being the source of his pleasure.

> I was a virgin, like a wall; now my breasts are like towers. When my lover looks at me, he is delighted with what he sees.
>
> —Song of Solomon 8:10

Men and women were uniquely designed. God created men to be visually stimulated by women, and he created women with physical form and beauty to attract the attention and delight of men. This is not a result of the fall but God's intended and beautiful design. When expressed appropriately within the bounds of marriage, this mutual delight mirrors the unity and intimacy of the Trinity.

While this particular application pertains to a husband and a wife, inviting delight is not exclusive to a marital relationship. All women are designed with a desire to be delighted in, to please, and to give pleasure. This can take many forms as a woman brings her own individuality to bear on the world around her. She may invite delight through her artistic expression or musical talent. It may be through her ability to make everyone she knows feel like they are the most important person in the room. Or it may be through her gift of hospitality. The applications are as varied and unique as the woman.

A woman delights to be delighted in, to be a source of pleasure. It is evident in her brightened countenance upon receiving a compliment. It is evident even in young girls. For example, many little girls like to play dress up, but often the fun of dressing up is not merely about creativity and playing imaginary roles. Part of the joy of dressing up is the affirmation received by an audience as she twirls and spins before those who may be watching.

Inviting delight can turn in on itself and become vanity and self-worship, but nevertheless, in its original creation and redeemed condition, the inviting impulse beats right from the heart of its Creator: God.

The idea that you were created as a source of delight for others may frustrate you, and you may feel that it trivializes or marginalizes you as a woman. You may also fear that you do not meet cultural standards of beauty, which may cause you to despair. Both reactions are based on a false understanding of beauty and delight. Both are rooted in self. True beauty, true delight is found in a woman who is fearfully and wonderfully made and who reflects the image of God within her. Being a source of delight to others is not marginalizing, nor is it weakness.

Any woman may glorify God by finding her sense of contentment and significance in Jesus. This makes her delightful, desirable to be around and to know. But she must never be deceived that she is the ultimate end of her allure. Those who "see" her need to "look through" her and treasure the One she reflects.

C.S. Lewis, in his work, *The Great Divorce,* describes a woman who embodies the heart of invitation:

> "Every young man or boy that met her became her son—even if it was only the boy that brought the meat to her back door.

> Every girl that met her was her daughter . . . But her motherhood was of a different kind. Those on whom it fell went back to their natural parents loving them more. Few men looked on her without becoming, in a certain fashion, her lovers. But it was the kind of love that made them not less true, but truer, to their own wives . . . Every beast and bird that came near her had its place in her love. In her they became themselves. And now the abundance of life she has in Christ from the Father flows over into them . . . Redeemed humanity is still young, it has hardly come to its full strength. But already there is joy enough in the little finger of a great saint such as yonder lady to waken all the dead things of the universe into life."[11]

Lewis's illustration gives insight into the essence of invitation in a woman. She is approachable, vulnerable, comforting, inclusive, and welcoming. Beauty radiates from within her. She brings delight. Others are drawn to her, desiring to be around her. Her presence is life giving. In her, they become themselves. She bids others to come find life, joy, peace, and rest. And invitation is where it begins.

Questions for Reflection

1. In what ways is God a source of delight?

2. How do you feel about being a source of delight to others? Why?

3. In what ways can you be a source of delight or pleasure for others? How has God uniquely equipped you to bring delight to those around you?

A GENTLE AND QUIET SPIRIT

IT'S NOT WHAT YOU THINK

Many women who hear the phrase "gentle and quiet spirit" associate it with a personality type, with a woman who is soft-spoken or timid. This thought frustrates many women as they feel the tension between who they are and who they think they are "supposed" to be. To be clear on the capacity of inviting, we must understand what it means to have a gentle and quiet spirit.

> In the same way, you wives must accept the authority of your husbands. Then, even if some refuse to obey the Good News, your godly lives will speak to them without any words. They will be won over by observing your pure and reverent lives. Don't be concerned about the outward beauty of fancy hairstyles, expensive jewelry, or beautiful clothes. You should clothe yourselves instead with the beauty that comes from within, the unfading beauty of a gentle and quiet spirit, which is so precious to God. This is how the holy women of old made themselves beautiful. They trusted God and accepted the authority of their husbands. For instance, Sarah obeyed her husband, Abraham, and called him her master. You are her

> daughters when you do what is right without fear of what your husbands might do.
>
> —1 Peter 3:1-6

The original audience of this passage was first century Christians living under the tyranny of the Roman government. In this passage, Peter addressed women in uncomfortable, even threatening situations, who were most likely married to unbelieving men. During this period, women were not held in high regard. They were often forced to take on the religions of their husbands and could be divorced without recourse. Yet, in spite of their uncomfortable circumstances, Peter exhorts them to respect the authority of their husbands. He calls them to live in such a way that even their unbelieving husbands could be won, not by words, but from the inward beauty of their lives. Although this passage is addressing married women, there are transcendent principles that have relevant application for all believing women today, regardless of marital status. It is important to note that this passage is not a command to ignore external beauty. There is nothing wrong with jewelry, dress, or hairstyles in and of themselves. But a woman's focus should not be merely on the surface. The idea of modesty is often misunderstood and boiled down to an issue of low necklines and high hemlines; however, true modesty is about more than clothing. Before modesty is reflected in dress, it is reflected in attitude. To be modest means you are not overly concerned with yourself. Modesty is freedom from vanity, egotism, boastfulness, and pretension. Modesty is reflected in an attitude of humility—in the elevation of others above self. This attitude will reflect itself in the way you dress as you seek to love others and in the way you present yourself in word, deed, and appearance.

Peter says women are to clothe themselves with a gentle and quiet spirit. There is often a misconception about the phrase "gentle and quiet spirit" which causes many women to bristle at the mere mention of it. A gentle and quiet spirit is not about being soft-spoken. It is not a personality type, nor is it a temperament. It is about being approachable and open to others, like a comfortable front porch that draws others to come to you and find rest. It is a God-given spirit, a disposition that gives women the capacity to welcome others into relationship with them. A quiet spirit makes a customized invitation, meeting others where they are. A quiet spirit draws others to a safe place.

In Greek, the word *gentle* is the same word Jesus used when he called himself meek and lowly, a word generally used to describe slaves.

> Take my yoke upon you, and learn from me, for I am gentle and lowly in heart, and you will find rest for your souls.
>
> —Matthew 11:29 (ESV)

Although Jesus was meek, he still spoke forthrightly. Jesus was not weak. He was bold. The word *gentle* denotes strength. Meekness is not weakness; it is strength with restraint. It is power under control. Jesus is the perfect example of this. All of the power of divinity was within him, yet he exhibited tremendous restraint of this power during his life on earth. He could be gentle because he entrusted himself to the One who judges righteously (1 Peter 2:23).

Being gentle and quiet does not mean a woman will never disagree with others. On the contrary, as disagreements occur, she will be wise and discerning in her responses. The book of James has much to say about the importance of taming the tongue. "The tongue is a small thing that makes grand speeches. But a tiny spark can set a great forest on fire" (James 3:5). The tongue is a powerful tool a woman can use to build others up or to tear them down. It is why the book of Proverbs says multiple times that it is better to live alone in the desert or on the corner of a roof than with a quarrelsome, complaining wife (Proverbs 19:13, 21:9, 21:19, 25:24, 27:15).

A woman with a gentle and quiet spirit recognizes that there is a time to speak clearly and boldly and a time to exercise restraint. Because she has a settled confidence in Christ, she has no need to prove herself. But when she does speak, kindness and wisdom are on her tongue (Proverbs 31:26). She does not need, in an unhealthy way, to be seen, noticed, or heard. Having a gentle spirit means she does not demand her own rights. Instead, the gentle spirit trusts in God's justice. Her security is found in knowing the One who is in control and trusting him. This confidence undergirds a woman's capacity to be inviting.

A woman with a gentle and quiet spirit is equipped in every way to be inviting and to bring delight. Men and women alike want to be in her presence. She holds herself loosely and as a result is teachable, always open to learn and to change. She is patient and forgiving toward others and herself. She has abandoned self-reliance, aware that she does not know what is truly good for her or for others. She has an inner core of satisfaction that is not dependent upon circumstances or others' opinions. She is accepting and non-judgmental because she sees herself as broken too. And she is able to laugh, especially at herself. She shows sincere interest in other people. She has a peace and settledness about her that is comforting and invites others to rest in her presence. But it's not about what she says or does; it is who she is within and her love for other people over herself. It is her humility and confidence in God that produces genuineness and vulnerability and frees her from the need to prove or defend herself.

None of this is about personality. It is the imprint of God on her character, and it flows from her relationship with him. She knows and believes in his goodness and mercy. She knows and believes that he is for her and she entrusts herself to him. She does not need to be self-protective because she knows the One who judges righteously. She does not need to prove herself or perform because she knows the One who has proven himself and performed ultimately.

The love, acceptance, and security she has found in God frees her to be vulnerable with others, to be courageous, and to take risks emotionally and relationally. She is free to be seen and known for who she really is—in all her weaknesses and failures—instead of desperately trying to be who she thinks others expect her to be. But not in a brash or brazen way that demands others accept her; rather, she exhibits a quiet confidence that makes others want to be in her presence. She is free to fail, to look foolish, to be rejected, to be exposed. All of this makes her desirable to be around because she provides others a safe place to be known in all their own weaknesses, insecurities, fears, failings, and need.

Being inviting is not a self-improvement plan or a fix-it list. Exerting control and trying to fix is not trusting; that is autonomy. You cannot fix the problem of being uninviting. However, you can get a vision for inviting based upon the gospel and move in that direction. This is a trajectory, not a place of arrival.

A gentle and quiet spirit is not a goal for you to achieve. The more you trust Christ, the more you will reflect his gentle and quiet spirit. It is, instead, centering on him. It is trusting in and finding satisfaction in God. A gentle and quiet spirit is the result of trusting that you are accepted and loved by God. In believing this, you make others feel accepted, welcomed, and at rest. You are inviting.

Questions for Reflection

1. What do you tend to think about when getting dressed each morning? How do your thoughts affect your clothing choices?

2. What does it look like for you to love others, both male and female, through your dress?

3. What is your reaction to the phrase "gentle and quiet spirit"? How is the actual definition different from what you previously imagined?

4. Where have you seen the capacity of inviting lived out well in another woman?

5. How could the freedom Christ offers enable you to be inviting, even to those who are hostile toward you?

HOW DOES AUTONOMY CORRUPT INVITING?

Women are designed with the capacity to honor the Lord by being inviting. But through the core sin of autonomy, invitation can be withdrawn in self-protection or extended to bring the focus to oneself through self-promotion. To err toward self-protection or self-promotion is part of a woman's broken nature, but it is possible to become inviting in a God-glorifying way. The gospel offers women freedom from bondage to sin.

Inviting in a way that reflects the heart of the Father is sacrificial and intentional. When you invite another, you hold yourself out to them and draw them in on their terms, not your own. It is a customized invitation to them based on who they are, what they need, and how you can best love and serve them. It requires you to be vulnerable, humble, and willing to engage them where they are.

Inviting is not forcing someone to move toward you; it is just being available to them. You may be rejected. But a woman who understands that Christ accepts her and loves her wholly need not fear rejection by humanity.

A woman who lives out of her abundance in Christ is free to invite others to partake of what she has to offer. She does not need to promote or protect herself, because her security rests in Jesus.

As image-bearers living out the capacity of inviting, women are to draw others in to bring glory to God. But often, that is not the destination to which we point them.

What are you inviting others into? Are you inviting them into your own world, full of fear, anxiety, frustration, and unrealistic expectations? Or are you, like Jesus, inviting them into a place of refuge, rest, and hope? Will your invitation be a source of comfort? Will they leave you feeling better than when they came to you? Will you reflect the inviting nature of God that soothes weary souls and satisfies the desolate? Will you point them to Christ or will you point them to self?

Will you consume them and lead them down the road of death or will you lead them to life in Christ? The corrupted expression of autonomy will be as varied as women are varied. Consider the triangle illustration from chapter 1. As you look at your individuality and your season of life, you can see not only how opportunities to invite look different, but also how your individuality affects the ways you corrupt the capacity of inviting.

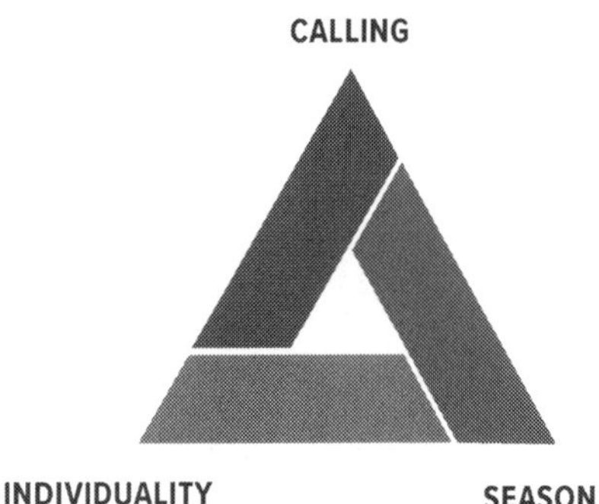

The applications for inviting are numerous and require you to reflect on your own individuality and season of life. By providing examples, we run the risk of creating caricatures and broad generalizations that may not be true of all women. However, as with any concept, it is often easier to gain understanding through stories or examples. The examples we provide are just that—examples. They may not be true in every case, but we feel they are helpful in illustrating these concepts.

Following are a few ways in which the capacity to invite others into relationship may be corrupted.

A WOMAN WHO . . .

A woman who surrounds herself with only people who are like her—those with similar interests, personalities, or seasons of life. Her invitation is not broad and inclusive, but selective and exclusive. This woman's idol is comfort and is a form of self-protection. She finds it easier and more comfortable to be around people who are like her because she does not have to extend herself or her energy to invite them into her world. She may be approaching relationships based on what they have to offer her, rather than what she may offer to another.

A woman who invites others into her world through gossip. This woman may feel a relational deficit, so she attempts to connect with others through the latest gossip or through a shared bond over a mutual enemy. This woman's idol is approval and is a form of self-promotion. She is driven by her need or lack, rather than by her desire to be a source to others.

A woman who finds it easier to be friends with men. She may feel threatened in the presence of other women or she may desire the affirmation she finds from being "one of the guys." This woman's need drives her to shut out the feminine gender in self-protection and creates a world that affirms her through self-promotion. She enjoys being the center of attention in her all-male world.

A woman who engages in premarital or extramarital sex. She is not inviting a man to live out his calling to take responsibility but is instead enabling him to remain a boy. Because of her quest for love or her desire to satisfy her appetites, she engages him in a way that fulfills her, albeit temporarily, and she consumes him for her own benefit. Her invitation leads him to destruction rather than life.

A woman who holds herself too tightly, either wrought with insecurities or thinking too highly of herself. Neither woman is available to hold herself out to others freely, openly, and without shame. Both women are enslaved to their own images and are unavailable to love and serve others well.

A woman who is insecure. She may close down in self-protection, not allowing others to get to know her for fear of how they may perceive her. She may surround herself with people who she thinks are less talented or personable in order to feel better about her own self. She may be guarded around people who aggravate her insecurities and keep them at arm's length—never allowing her to fully engage them.

A woman who struggles with her own body image or sees herself as overweight. She is not free to invite others because she has closed in on herself, withdrawing from relationships with men or women who may heighten these feelings of failure to measure up. She is never truly free to draw others into her world.

A woman who draws others to herself through the way she dresses. She may seek male attention by wearing clothes that are revealing, or female attention by wearing clothes that cause others to envy her. Her desire to self-promote isolates others and elevates herself.

A woman who is easily offended, hurt, or rattled by other people. She responds either by being critical, harsh, brusque, prickly, or aloof toward them or she becomes withdrawn, isolated, and unwilling to be vulnerable in order to avoid being hurt.

A woman who has been wounded in previous relationships and has closed in on herself in self-protection. Her fear of being hurt again and desire for assurances cause her to be unapproachable and withdrawn relationally and emotionally. She is unwilling to risk being vulnerable with others and is afraid that if anyone really knew her, she would be rejected again. She believes it is better to disengage and distance herself from others than it is to suffer the pain that relationships may bring.

A woman who doesn't want to call attention to herself or be in the center of conversations because she thinks it immodest and too forward. Rather than engaging others and loving them well, she sits back quietly and waits for them to engage her.

As a woman created in God's image, you have the opportunity to reflect the inviting aspect of his character to the world around you. To invite another into relationship is first and foremost about your Creator—honoring his image displayed through you. It is not about you. *You love, you invite, because he first loved and invited you.*

The Creator of all things has been engaged and engaging since the beginning, and he will be for all eternity. From Adam to Abraham, from Rahab to Ruth, from Israel to the Gentiles—his invitation is not just collective; it is personalized. He knows your name. He knows every hair on your head. He hears you when you pray, and he hears you when all you can do is groan. He knows what you need. He knows your strengths and weaknesses, your successes and failures. He knows everything about you. And he invites you to himself.

Invitation is where it begins, but it doesn't end there. Because of your invitation to others, you have a platform in their lives through which you can nurture and partner.

Questions for Reflection

1. In what ways do you see the capacity of inviting corrupted in your own life? When and how do you self-protect? When and how do you self-promote?

2. When is it difficult for you to be inviting? When is it easier?

3. What underlying issues (such as fears, insecurity, body image, control issues, past experiences, personality, and temperament) are your greatest obstacles to be inviting?

BIBLICAL PORTRAITS

INVITING CORRUPTED: DELILAH

READ JUDGES 16:1–22

In Judges 16, Samson fell in love with a woman named Delilah and became subject to her influence over him. After being promised money by the Philistine rulers in exchange for the secret to Samson's power, Delilah chose to use her influence over Samson for selfish gain. While we see strength, boldness, and resolve in Delilah, she acted autonomously, using these capacities instead to satisfy her own agenda. Lacking in humility and selflessness, her God-given capacity to be inviting was corrupted and perverted. Invitation became her weapon against Samson. Nagging him day after day, she wore him down. She did not ennoble Samson, nor did she lend him strength in his calling as a Nazirite (one committed to a vow of holy consecration requiring specific codes of conduct). She did not provide him with rest or a place to be vulnerable. Instead, she leveraged her influence in his life as a way to gain control over him, wear him down, and ultimately destroy him.

INVITING CORRUPTED: NAOMI

READ RUTH 1:1–22

In the book of Ruth, we are introduced to Naomi. Embittered by the loss of her husband and two sons, Naomi withdrew and moved into self-protection. Rather than embracing a new season as matriarch to her two daughters-in-law, Ruth and Orpah, she pushed them away. Naomi urged them to return to their families of origin. Upon returning to Bethlehem, the women of the town clamored, "Is this Naomi?" But Naomi, whose name means pleasant, insisted they no longer call her Naomi, but call her Mara, which means bitter. Naomi's grief over the loss of her husband and sons was legitimate. But, in her grief, she turned in on herself and her grief gave way to despair, and she became prickly and unapproachable to those around her. In verses 20b-21a, she blames God for her circumstances saying, "the Almighty has made life very bitter for me. I went away full, but the Lord has brought me back empty." Naomi's hope had been in something temporal rather than something transcendent. She placed security, hope, and identity in her roles as a wife and mother. As a result, Naomi found herself feeling empty, bitter, and hopeless.

INVITING REDEEMED: MARY, THE MOTHER OF JESUS

READ LUKE 1:26–56, 2:1–52

We do not have many details on the life of Mary, the mother of Jesus. Much of the information we do have has been gathered through historical context. Mary was likely from a poor family and was probably twelve to fourteen years of age when she was betrothed to Joseph. According to custom, Joseph and his family likely paid a dowry to secure Mary's hand in marriage. Though they had not yet had a marriage ceremony or consummated their marriage, Mary was already considered Joseph's wife. Imagine her surprise when an angel of the Lord appeared proclaiming that she, a virgin, would have a child—and not by her husband. This could have meant dire consequences for Mary. She could have been declared an adulteress. The consequences of adultery were, at best, public shame, divorce, loss of all rights accrued from the marriage settlement, and/or being cut off from her people. At worst, adultery, according to Mosaic Law, was punishable by death (Leviticus 20:10).

Any young girl in her situation would likely be terrified, yet that is not the response we see in Scripture. In Luke 1:38b (ESV), after being told she would give birth to a child, Mary said, "Behold, I am the servant of the Lord; let it be to me according to your word." In this brief declaration, Mary displays a gentle and quiet spirit that is rooted in her confidence and belief in the goodness of the God of Israel. She did not cower or shy away from potential suffering, grief, or conflict. Rather than becoming self-protective or seeking to defend herself, Mary entrusted herself to the care of God. She displayed a willing, humble submission to his redemptive plan despite the fact that it may cause her great difficulty. Mary not only willingly submitted to God's plan, but when visiting Elizabeth, she burst into a song of praise declaring the great things God had done for her. She had a disposition and posture of deep gratitude in spite of her less than desirable circumstance.

We also see her gentle and quiet spirit on display when the shepherds came to see baby Jesus in Luke 2. After they recounted the story of the angel of the Lord telling them Jesus was the Savior of the world, we are told "Mary treasured up all these things and pondered them in her heart" (v. 19 ESV). She did not promote herself, telling others she just gave birth to the Christ. She did not find identity, satisfaction, worth, or pride in her role as mother of the Messiah. Rather, recognizing her own need for God's grace and salvation, she displayed a humble reverence for the Lord. And as Matthew Henry explains it, just as she "had silently left it to God to clear up her virtue, when that was suspected, so she silently leaves it to him to publish her honour, now when it was veiled; and it is satisfaction enough to find that, if no one else takes notice of the birth of her child, angels do."[12] Ultimately, Mary's disposition was inviting because she believed God and entrusted herself to his loving, faithful care.

Questions for Reflection

1. What are some other examples from the Bible or your own life that illustrate the capacity of inviting in positive ways?

2. What examples from the Bible or your own life illustrate negative ways to invite?

04

NURTURING

In the last chapter, we discussed the core capacity of inviting. Because a woman's core calling occurs within the context of relationship, inviting serves as the gateway through which she can nurture and partner. In this chapter, we will explore the core capacity of nurturing.

The essence and goal of nurturing is to take frail, vulnerable life and create an environment where this life can come to full intended form. However, it is important to note that all people are in need. Even those who appear strong and seemingly have it all together benefit from being nurtured.

Nurturing is caring for and encouraging the development of another in a way that creates strength in them and enables them to flourish. The goal of nurturing is maturity and independence, to bring strength to bear on another in a way that launches them and enables them to succeed.

THE NURTURING NATURE OF GOD

From the very beginning, as God created the world, he revealed himself as a nurturer. The garden he formed was a place where mankind could flourish—an environment where man and woman could become everything he intended them to be (Genesis 2:8–9a). God not only created this environment but also took great care to maintain his creation (Job 38–41).

And in God's great mercy and kindness, he not only nurtures on a universal scale but also nurtures us personally. He is intimately involved with the details of your life. He knows every need, every weakness, every area of concern.

> That is why I tell you not to worry about everyday life—whether you have enough food and drink, or enough clothes to wear. Isn't life more than food, and your body more than clothing? Look at the birds. They don't plant or harvest or store food in barns, for your heavenly Father feeds them. And aren't you far more valuable to him than they are? Can all your worries add a single moment to your life? And why worry about your clothing? Look at the lilies of the field and how they grow. They don't work or make their clothing, yet Solomon in all his glory was not dressed as beautifully as they are. And if God cares so wonderfully for wildflowers that are here today and thrown into the fire tomorrow, he will certainly care for you. Why do you have so little faith? So don't worry about these things, saying, "What will we eat? What will we drink? What will we wear?" These things dominate the thoughts of unbelievers, but your heavenly Father already knows all your needs. Seek the Kingdom of God above all else, and live righteously, and he will give you everything you need.
>
> —Matthew 6:25–33

The divine attribute of nurturing is on brilliant display in God's loving design to nourish and care for humanity. The story of Scripture from beginning to end reveals a God who cares for, loves, and nurtures his children. He looks on his children, vulnerable and needy, and invites them to come to him to find the strength and nourishment they desperately need (Isaiah 55:1–3a).

Questions for Reflection

1. In what ways does God nurture? Where do you see God nurturing you?

2. How does God's nurture provide you with strength and life?

A SOURCE OF LIFE

Nurturing cannot be divorced from the idea of giving life. A woman's body is physically designed to nurture. She was created in such a way that she could receive a seed and innately nurture and engender life. Further, she sustains that life for another twelve months outside of the womb through nursing. Her body is able to take a vulnerable life and bring it to full form. This physical feminine makeup is emblematic of her nurturing capacity.

Many women reading this material may have one of several reactions to this point. First, many may have very painful experiences with the idea of childbearing or nursing. In this fallen world, your body may betray you. Infertility is a reality for many women. Exploring the life-giving aspect of nurturing may be painful to you in your unmet desire to conceive or nurse children. Or you may be single and feel that your capacity to nurture cannot be recognized apart from childbearing. This simply is not true. It is important to remember that your circumstances, whether infertility or singleness, do not nullify your capacity to nurture. Bearing children is not essential for reflecting the image of God through nurturing. One may be nurturing while mothering, but one need not be a mother to be nurturing.

Finally, there may be some women who find the idea that women were created for childbearing antiquated, belittling, and repressive. This seems to be a common thought among younger women today, particularly on many college campuses. You may feel that motherhood is a waste of a woman's intelligence, education, and talents, and as such is not a worthwhile pursuit.

Regardless of your personal view on this topic, it is undeniable that the physiological design of the female body nurtures, sustains, and strengthens life in a way that the male body cannot. It is important to resist the temptation to devalue, create a caricature, or attempt to move beyond this capacity. A woman's body symbolically represents the nurturing attribute of God.

However, we must remember that life season and individuality do not dictate if the core capacity of nurturing is present, only how it is expressed. Historically, the word *nurture* has denoted the act of nursing, to suckle or nourish.[13] In the book of Isaiah, the Lord uses this same language to illustrate his care for and love of Israel:

> Sing for joy, O heavens! Rejoice, O earth!
>
> Burst into song, O mountains!
>
> For the Lord has comforted his people
>
> and will have compassion on them in their suffering. Yet Jerusalem says, "The Lord has deserted us;
>
> the Lord has forgotten us."
>
> Never! Can a mother forget her nursing child? Can she feel no love for the child she has borne? But even if that were possible,

> I would not forget you!
>
> See, I have written your name on the palms of my hands.
> Always in my mind is a picture of Jerusalem's walls in ruins.
>
> —Isaiah 49:13–16

Israel, the people of the Lord, felt forgotten and abandoned in their suffering. But the Lord looked on them—vulnerable, frail, and needy—like an infant still nursing at its mother's breast, and he comforted and encouraged them using maternal imagery.

It is undeniable that women have the unique capacity to provide much needed nourishment and sustenance to a vulnerable and needy child. The unborn child receives everything needed from the mother to fully develop into a self-sustainable life. The nursing child receives necessary nutrients and antibodies through the mother's breast milk. Nursing not only provides for a child's physical needs, it provides for the baby's mental and emotional needs as well. While nursing, the bonding hormone oxytocin is released, helping the child feel comforted, safer, and more relaxed.

When growing life within her or nursing a child, a mother provides the nourishment her child needs, and at the same time she depletes her own body. She sacrificially gives of her body and resources for the nourishment and strengthening of another. She is a consumable. In every way, she is supplying the child with everything needed for a healthy life. However, as the baby develops, gaining in strength and independence, weaning becomes the goal.

We see a similar picture of sacrificial nurturing in the New Testament. In John chapter 6, Jesus holds himself out as the true nourishment Israel needs, referring to himself as "the bread of life" (vs. 47–51). Jesus compares himself to the manna the early Israelites ate in the desert. All those who ate the manna eventually died, but Jesus declares that anyone who eats the bread he gives will live. Jesus sees the plight of Israel and us, and he holds himself out to all as a source of life.

But there is perhaps no more compelling picture of the heart of nurturing than that of Jesus Christ at the Last Supper:

> When the time came, Jesus and the apostles sat down together at the table. Jesus said, "I have been very eager to eat this Passover meal with you before my suffering begins. For I tell you now that I won't eat this meal again until its meaning is fulfilled in the Kingdom of God."
>
> Then he took a cup of wine and gave thanks to God for it. Then he said, "Take this and share it among yourselves. For I will not drink wine again until the Kingdom of God has come."
>
> He took some bread and gave thanks to God for it. Then he broke it in pieces and gave it to the disciples, saying, "This is my body, which is given for you. Do this to remember me."
>
> After supper he took another cup of wine and said, "This cup is the new covenant between God and his people—an agreement confirmed with my blood, which is poured out as a sacrifice for you."
>
> —Luke 22:14–20

Jesus Christ, who was with God from the beginning of the world, became flesh and blood for us (John 1:1–4). Though he was fully God in every way, Jesus humbled himself, giving up his divine privilege, and was born into the loneliness, suffering, and temptation of this world. He learned obedience as a son, humbled himself in obedience to God, and died a criminal's death on a cross in order that we might live (Philippians 2:6–8).

This passage in Luke is during Jesus' final Passover meal with his disciples at the end of his three-year ministry. Anticipating his arrest and crucifixion, Jesus gathers his disciples for this feast in which all of Israel remembers the Lord's deliverance from slavery in Egypt (Exodus 12). But this meal was different than all others before. Jesus broke the bread, and as he gave it to his disciples, he declared, "This is my body, which is given for you." And then he passed the cup of wine, saying, "This cup is the new covenant between God and his people—an agreement confirmed with my blood, which is poured out as a sacrifice for you."

This is perhaps the most glorious display of a nurturing heart. Jesus Christ became a consumable. His body was broken and his blood was poured out to bring life, comfort, hope, security, and nourishment to frail, vulnerable, weak people. His life, death, and resurrection make life possible for all who believe in him. Communion, or the Lord's Supper, serves as a tangible reminder of God's grace as poured out through Jesus. Communion provides believers with spiritual nourishment that feeds and strengthens their hungry, weary souls. It is truly good for the heart to be strengthened by grace (Hebrews 13:9).

Jesus' commitment to nurturing humanity was sacrificial and costly. His life became your life. His inheritance became your inheritance. His status became your status. His resources and strength became your resources and strength. And through this divine act of nurturing, Christ enabled you to become more of who God created you to be. This is the very heart of nurturing. But what does nurturing look like in the day-to-day life of a woman? Practically, how is a woman a "consumable" and a source of life for another? We'll explore these questions in the next section.

Questions for Reflection

1. Have you ever thought about communion as nurturing? How might this understanding change the way you view and take communion?

2. Whether or not you are a mother, where can you see evidence of a capacity to nurture in your life?

NURTURING IN THE LIFE OF A WOMAN

The capacity of nurturing has been largely misunderstood and misrepresented as weak and insignificant. Nurturing is not weak and insignificant, nor is it a personality type. Nurturing is a significant, self-sacrificing, and God-reflecting attribute. Women were created to undergird or bring strength to others.

To reflect the image of God through nurturing is to give of yourself sacrificially for the benefit of another. Nurturing occurs in a variety of ways and relationships and is always intended to grow another for the purpose of launching them to serve God in the way he designed them. When a woman nurtures, she empowers and encourages others, helping them feel stronger, bolder, more capable, and more of who God created them to be.

The essence of nurturing is life giving. A woman who allows herself to become a consumable for another recognizes his or her frailty and brings all she is to bear on that person. She does this not in a belittling, arrogant way, but in a way that affirms. She brings all of her individuality (talents, resources, life experience, energy) alongside another and allows the other person to feed from her in a way that produces life, strength, and development.

A baby in the safety of the mother's womb receives life-giving nourishment that allows development in a way that is sustainable outside the mother's womb. From conception, the child is growing in strength and independence, preparing to live wholly apart from her. Likewise, to nurture is to develop others, to provide something they need, not in a way that makes them dependent on you, but in a way that makes them strong. Nurturing develops another through fostering, training, equipping, and empowering.

For example, let's consider a young woman who has no family to speak of and has never had good role models. Through a series of sins committed against her, as well as sins of her own choosing, the young woman is lost, alone, and struggling.

An older woman sees this frail life and not only invites her into relationship, but also invites her into her own home. For months, the older woman gives her time, energy, and resources to equip and train the younger woman to succeed. The end result is that the young woman becomes stronger, more independent, and able to live and make healthy choices on her own.

Nurturing is not self-centered; it comes from a posture of humility. To nurture like Christ involves a willingness to humble yourself and deplete your resources, your energy, and your life on the behalf of another. Nurturing is loving others well at your own expense.

It is not patronizing or accidental. It requires wisdom and strength. It requires knowledge, thought, and action. When healthy, nurturing creates an environment where dependence is temporary and culminates in maturity.

We must resist the temptation to diminish nurturing to a caricature. Nurturing is not about baking cookies and kissing boo-boos, though that may be part of it. It is a powerful, God-given capacity that will be expressed differently in each woman based on her individuality and season of life. For example, when her child falls and scrapes a knee, a mother who says, "You're okay. Brush it off. You can keep playing," may have trouble believing she is nurturing. However, this mother is communicating to her child that she believes her child is capable and strong. Her nurturing empowers and instills confidence that the child has the ability to handle the situation.

Just as the expression of inviting varies from woman to woman, so does nurturing. Nurturing may include mentoring relationships, biological children, adopted children, spiritual children, students, aging or ill parents, coworkers, or any number of possible relationships.

In order to nurture well, it is important to understand the person you are nurturing. This takes time and requires listening to them, asking questions, and seeking to understand them and what makes them tick. It requires a posture of humility, knowing that it is not about you. A big part of nurturing is knowing who they are and what will strengthen, empower, encourage, and equip them to be who God created them to be.

For example, not all students learn the same way. When a teacher takes the time to learn and understand each student's strengths and weaknesses, she is better equipped to nurture. Understanding that one student may learn better by listening and taking notes, while another may learn better through hands-on activity, she is able to integrate a variety of educational methods that better equip each student to succeed.

The capacity of nurture is also present when a woman reaches out to someone who is broken, vulnerable, and in deep need. For example, a single woman is invited to a neighborhood Bible study. During the first group meeting, the young woman confides in her peers that she is pregnant. Rather than scorning her, dismissing her, or distancing themselves from her, the women move toward her. They seek to learn about her situation—discovering that her parents have disowned her and her boyfriend wants her to have an abortion. She, on the other hand, believes that she needs to keep the baby.

Throughout the Bible study, these women love her with grace and truth; they help her navigate tough choices; they help her do research on resources that are available to her; they help her learn what repentance looks like in her life; and they act as accountability partners as she learns how to follow Jesus and resist the temptations of sexual sin. They even throw her a baby shower and help her prepare to become a single mom. These women do not condone or ignore her choice to have premarital sex. But rather than abandoning her in her sin and moment of need, they rally to her and help her mentally, emotionally, physically, and spiritually. As a result, she is stronger, more capable, and better prepared for this new season of her life. And better yet, she has a community of godly women who are there for her and keep pointing her toward truth.

Nurturing people well also requires you to let them know your sin and weakness. To not do so could mean that you do more harm than good. If you are unwilling to allow them to see your frailty, they may feel inferior and be afraid to be known in their weakness. This relationship, built on false pretense, is not a safe place for them to disclose their sins and struggles. By reminding them of your own weakness and need, you free them to be who they are and to receive help from another.

Further, if you imply that you have it all together, they may not know how to go to Christ to find strength and may instead place you on a pedestal as their functional savior. You have to show them how you rely on Christ. As you live out dependence on him, you lead them to depend on him. The goal of nurturing is not to create dependence on you. That is not sustainable or healthy. The goal of nurturing is to create an opportunity for another to be strengthened in a way that eventually makes them less dependent on you. You want to come alongside and urge them to depend on Christ.

Like the other capacities, nurturing has countless expressions. Nurturing extends to the simplest acts of love. A woman who offers a kind word, a smile, a warm embrace, or a listening ear is experiencing and exhibiting her capacity to nurture. Nurturing can even extend to strangers through meaningful interaction. As a woman encourages, empowers, and brings life to someone else, she acts from the heart of nurturing femininity.

Questions for Reflection

1. When you consider your individuality and season, what are some relationships in which you are using your nurturing capacity?

2. How is nurturing different from how you may have previously thought of it?

3. Where have you seen this capacity lived out well in another woman?

4. How could you nurture those in a position of authority over you? How about those who seem to be strong enough on their own?

RUTH

AN UNEXPECTED PICTURE OF NURTURING

One of the most beautiful examples of redeemed nurturing can be found in the book of Ruth. In this Old Testament book, we discover Ruth nurturing her mother-in-law, Naomi. It is a beautiful picture of this capacity in a context we would not typically expect.

The events in this book took place during the time of the judges. It was a dark time in Israel's history, a time of wickedness when the Israelites prostituted themselves to other gods and worshiped them. "Everyone did what was right in his own eyes" (Judges 21:25b ESV). There was also famine in the land. In an effort to provide for his family, Elimelech moved his wife, Naomi, and his two sons to the land of Moab. The Moabite people originated from an incestuous relationship between Lot and his oldest daughter. There was much history between Moab and Israel that resulted in disdain for one another. Throughout history, the Moabites attacked and oppressed the Israelites; tension between the two lands ran deep.

While living in Moab, Naomi's husband, Elimelech, died. Her sons married Moabite women named Ruth and Orpah. While this was not against the law, it was highly discouraged due to the Moabites' worship of other gods. Ten years later, both of Naomi's sons died, leaving her with no one to provide for her and her daughters-in-law. Widowed, childless, and with no means of financial support in a hostile land, Naomi decided to return to her hometown of Bethlehem.

Though Ruth and Orpah were legally bound to her, Naomi freed them to return to their own families and their own gods. Both women initially resisted, but after further chiding, Orpah turned back. Ruth, however, clung to her mother-in-law. Though Naomi had nothing to offer her, Ruth displayed deep loyalty to Naomi, declaring, "Don't ask me to leave you and turn back. Wherever you go, I will go; wherever you live, I will live. Your people will be my people, and your God will be my God. Wherever you die, I will die, and there I will be buried" (Ruth 1:16b-17a).

Naomi and Ruth journeyed a difficult road, physically, spiritually, and emotionally. Naomi was bitter, depressed, and hopeless. She believed the hand of the Lord was against her. In contrast was Ruth: a widowed, barren, poor foreigner. In spite of the ridicule she faced as an outsider in Israeli territory, the potential hardship that lay ahead, and Naomi's less than inviting disposition, Ruth was steadfast in her commitment to nurture Naomi.

Upon entering Bethlehem, Ruth provided for Naomi by taking advantage of the Levitical law that allowed widows and the impoverished to glean the fields behind the harvesters (Leviticus 19:9). Traditionally, men would cut the wheat, and women would walk behind them gathering the grain in bundles. The law given to Moses declared that the corners and edges of the field should be left untouched by the harvesters so the widows and poor could collect and feed themselves. Yet, Ruth did not just accept what she was allowed by law to do. Instead, in an effort to care for Naomi, Ruth boldly asked permission to glean along with the others behind the harvesters.

As it happens, Ruth was gleaning in the field of Boaz, a close relative of Naomi. Boaz honored Ruth's boldness, and through him, the grace of God was poured onto Ruth. Boaz allowed Ruth to glean behind his harvesters, directed his men not to embarrass her, and provided her with food and water. Ruth labored until evening, and then she threshed the barley and carried twenty-nine pounds of grain home to Naomi. The abundance took Naomi by surprise. Discovering the favor Boaz had bestowed upon Ruth, Naomi found renewed hope and devised a plan to help Ruth secure Boaz as a husband. By directing Ruth to go to the threshing floor and lay at Boaz's feet as he slept, Naomi was, in essence, directing Ruth to proposition Boaz for marriage. This was an appeal to Levitical law which declared that the nearest relative of a widow had a responsibility to marry and care for her (Deuteronomy 25:5–6).

Ruth listened to her mother-in-law's instructions, went to the threshing floor, uncovered Boaz's feet, and lay down.

When he discovered her, she appealed to him as a kinsman-redeemer, asking him to spread the corner of his blanket over her. This was not a love story. Ruth was asking Boaz to redeem the land of Naomi's family and to provide an heir to carry on Naomi's family name. Ruth placed herself in a vulnerable position, risking her reputation. She did not wait for Boaz to be noble or generous. Instead, she invited him to be the man God had created him to be. She emboldened him to act, to move into this hard situation and make it better.

It was a bold move on Naomi's behalf. Boaz recognized this saying, "The Lord bless you, my daughter! . . . You are showing even more family loyalty now than you did before, for you have not gone after a younger man, whether rich or poor. Now don't worry about a thing, my daughter. I will do what is necessary for everyone in town knows you are a virtuous woman" (Ruth 3:10–11).

This Moabite woman, of less than respectable origins, was hailed a virtuous woman by a well-respected Israelite man. In the end, Boaz married Ruth and provided her with a son. That son's name was Obed. Obed was the father of Jesse. Jesse was the father of King David, the line from which Jesus the Messiah would come.

WHAT DOES RUTH TEACH US ABOUT NURTURING?

We discover, through Ruth's example, that nurturing is a powerful agent of change when employed for God's purposes. It is a divine attribute that is intentional and intelligent. Ruth was not weak or passive, nor was she resigned to her circumstances. She was fully engaged.

Ruth recognized Naomi's weakness and vulnerability, and she responded by coming alongside Naomi with strength and diligence. Ruth could have taken the easier way and returned to her family, but she didn't. Instead, she took an active role in nurturing her mother-in-law. She did not shrink back in fear of what it may cost her. On the contrary, she put herself in danger to help.

At the beginning of the book of Ruth, Naomi was bitter and resigned to her circumstances. By the middle of the story, Naomi was stronger and began to nurture Ruth by helping her with Boaz. And by the end of the book, Naomi cared for Ruth's son, Obed, as if he were her own (Ruth 4:16). Through the nourishment and nurturing that Ruth provided, Naomi became more of the *ezer* God created her to be. By utilizing her God-given capacity to nurture, Ruth led Naomi from a place of despair to renewed hope, from a place of weakness and need to a place of strength. Because Ruth did not cling tightly to protecting or promoting herself but gave of herself sacrificially, Naomi moved from a place of humiliation to exaltation, hailed by the women of the town (Ruth 4:14–17).

Generations were changed because of Ruth's boldness. She demonstrated that nurturing is not reserved for motherhood as she nurtured both Naomi and Boaz. What we see in the book of Ruth is that it is not always easy to be an *ezer*. Sometimes you must be an *ezer* to difficult people and in less than ideal circumstances. Yet the call as God's image-bearers applies in difficult situations, not just ideal ones.
At times, it will require great risk and sacrifice as you place yourself in a position where another could hurt you. In his book *Tempted and Tried*, Russell Moore states:

> "Risk is inherent in every kind of other-directed life . . . Courage isn't protecting yourself in a cocoon from these possibilities. Courage is walking forward and embracing others in love even though you may suffer greatly in ways you could never imagine now. Jesus walked that way before you, and he walks that way with you now. That's the way of the cross."[14]

Question for Reflection

1. What do you learn about nurturing from Ruth's example?

HOW DOES AUTONOMY CORRUPT NURTURING?

God created and entrusted women with the capacity to nurture in order to bring him glory and to benefit others. Nurturing, like the other capacities, focuses outwardly on the needs of others, but autonomy twists these capacities and focuses them inwardly. Autonomy corrupts what God created. Whether consciously or not, nurturing in its corrupted form often puts self in the center through self-promotion or self-protection.

You were created as an essential counterpart, to bring strength and meet need through your relationship with others. Nurturing corrupted tends toward control—whether control over others or control over self. When nurturing, women may struggle either with being overly responsible and controlling in the lives of others (a form of self-promotion) or with being passive and abdicating responsibility in the lives of others (a form of self-protection).

CONCERN VERSUS RESPONSIBILITY

The following illustration, from *Instruments in the Redeemer's Hands* by Paul Tripp, may be a helpful tool as you attempt to discern what you are responsible for and what is just a concern.[15]

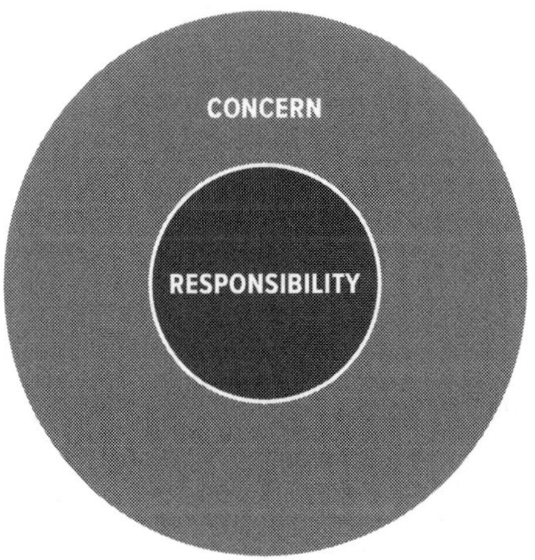

CONCERN (Entrust to God): The outer circle represents things that concern you but are beyond your ability and thus not your responsibility. These things must be identified and entrusted to God.

RESPONSIBILITY (Faithfully Obey): The inner circle represents the things God has called you to do that you cannot pass off to anyone else. The only proper response is to seek to understand and faithfully obey.

A **responsibility** is something that only you can do in a particular situation or relationship. This responsibility cannot and should not be passed on to someone else. In every relationship and situation, you must examine what God has called you personally to do. What is your responsibility?

A **concern** is a situation or person that is legitimate and important to you but is beyond or outside your abilities. You must identify concerns and entrust them to God. Concerns require humble acknowledgement of your limitations and trust in a faithful and sovereign God.

For example, you may be in a discipleship relationship with a woman whose marriage is failing. Perhaps she has even indicated that she is no longer interested in trying to make the marriage work. Your responsibility as one in a nurturing, discipleship relationship with her is to listen to her, ask her questions, challenge her, and speak truth to her, and perhaps even give her some direction to seek out counseling or pastoral care within her church. It is easy to be tempted to believe that you play a crucial role in the survival of her marriage, but you are not responsible for her choices or her marriage—this is a concern, which you must entrust to God. If you are fighting for her marriage harder than she is, then you have likely moved a legitimate concern into your circle of responsibility.

However, another situation may require you to do more than ask questions and listen. You may be in a season of life in which your parents are ill or aging. There may come a time when they are no longer able to take care of themselves. Senility has perhaps taken away their ability to even think or choose for themselves. In a situation such as this, it may be your responsibility to determine your parents' direction and future.

There are two temptations women may face regarding their capacity to nurture. First, you may be tempted to expand the inner circle and make responsibilities out of things that are concerns. Acting in autonomy, a woman may extend herself into the realm of concern and assume responsibility that is not hers to bear. But moving beyond the bounds of responsibility is not trusting God; it is trying to take control.

The second temptation is to shrink the inner circle of responsibility, abdicating your responsibility and creating an expectation that God will do what he already called you to do. God will empower you to do the things he has called you to do, but he will not do them for you.[16] To abdicate responsibility is not being obedient in your capacity to nurture. However, there are times when someone's situation may be serious and requires you to refer her to a professional. To do so is not an abdication of your responsibility.

It is also important to remember that understanding concern versus responsibility as it pertains to your life is a lifelong process. There is not a checklist for every woman to know what qualifies as a responsibility or concern. These circles are also fluid, with situations and people moving in and out of them on a constant basis. A good question to ask as you seek discernment between responsibility and concern is, "Will Jesus hold me accountable for this?" As an individual, it is not always easy to discern between concern and responsibility, but biblical community with other believers can often bring clarity to situations that are otherwise unclear. Wisdom and discernment grow within the context of community. But even as you seek community to help you discern your responsibility, there is still personal accountability to go to the Lord for guidance.

As with inviting, the corrupted expression of nurture will vary from woman to woman and situation to situation. It is important to reflect on your own individuality and season of life as you seek to understand the ways in which you may corrupt the capacity to nurture. Please remember that the examples we provide are not applicable in every case. They are merely meant to be helpful tools to illustrate ways in which nurturing may be corrupted.

Following are a few ways in which the capacity to nurture may be corrupted:

A WOMAN WHO . . .

A woman who has the spiritual gift of mercy, but the corruption of nurturing twists her use of this gift. She becomes a magnet for needy people. She offers a listening ear, counsel, and assistance, and in return, she is validated and affirmed by feeling needed and important. As a result, she never launches anyone. Rather than creating an environment where maturity and independence is the result, she perpetuates dependency. In this self-promoting way, she has leveraged her power to put herself at the center of relationships. In these situations, she is not pouring into others, but elevating herself. She is not bringing them strength, but is instead feeding on their weaknesses in order to make herself feel strong.

A woman who doesn't want to get involved in the messiness of others' lives. Because her idol is comfort, she withdraws whenever things get difficult or her friends and family are going through hard times. She is unwilling to bring her time, energy, and resources to bear on them in a way that strengthens and fortifies them. Instead, she self-protects, guarding herself from getting too heavily involved.

A woman who keeps her son or daughter unduly dependent upon her. Her value is in her role of motherhood, so she refuses to lose her worth by releasing her child. She does not nurture to prepare her children for their adult years. Instead, she debilitates them by doing everything for them. Alleviating their responsibility, she hinders her children's development in favor of fostering her own desires to be needed. As a result, her children are unprepared and relationally encumbered as she fails to launch them.

A woman who avoids conflict at all costs. She will not speak hard truth to her friends, enabling them to become more of who God created them to be, because she fears upsetting them or losing their friendship. She is more concerned with her need for approval and protecting her relationship with them than with their ultimate spiritual, mental, emotional, or physical well-being.

A woman who attempts to help her children succeed by forcing them into her self-determined mold. She does not take the time to learn who they are, what their interests and talents are, and how she may foster these. Rather, she pushes them to pursue activities or interests that she thinks are suitable. She does not take into consideration her son's academic excellence and interest in science and, in response, facilitate an environment where he may develop in these areas. She instead forces him to pursue sports like football and basketball with "all the other kids." She is not nurturing him. She is instead elevating her agenda over his individuality.

A woman who can't deal with weakness in others. Anytime she gets around someone who needs her, she begins to withdraw. She wants only friends who are peers. And even more than that, she hates needy men. She only wants to receive a man who is strong. She rejects the idea that men need help. In her perception, need is failure. Because her idol is comfort, she shuts down her availability and denies her calling as "essential counterpart."

A woman who panics when her husband loses a job or when something goes wrong with her children. Her reaction is often based in her own fears, which either paralyze her into inaction or spin her into a frenzied rush to control. Either way, she is unavailable to nurture and provide strength. Rather than expressing confidence in her husband's ability to handle the situation, thereby empowering, ennobling, and strengthening him, her fears, insecurities, and lack of trust in God and her husband communicate a lack of belief in him that deflates and discourages him instead.

A woman who thinks too highly of her abilities or importance and has not acknowledged her limitations. She rushes to the aid of others in an attempt to save them. But eventually, the dependence of others that was once so validating becomes too much to bear. The expectations of others ends up being oppressive because she is not wired to be God. Her idol of influence has paralyzed her ability to nurture. Finally realizing she cannot fulfill the unrealistic expectations of others, her temptation is to abandon her dependent relationships.

A woman who neglects the needs of her husband and children because it is more rewarding to help others. This woman may find the day-to-day tasks of picking up socks and grocery shopping mundane. She thinks it more pious to talk to a woman who is struggling with an issue than to nurture her husband by sitting beside him while he watches football. Everyone around her may speak well of her, while her family is starving for the nourishment only she can provide them.

A woman who has launched all of her children into adulthood and now finds herself in a new, lonely season of life. All of her children are gone and don't need her as they once did, and now she struggles to find a sense of purpose and direction for her life. Because most of her nurturing energy for the last twenty years has been directed toward her children, she is no longer sure how to relationally connect with her spouse. This leaves her floundering even more for the connection she once knew and tempts her to meddle or be overly concerned and involved with the lives of her children and grandchildren. This only further isolates her as her adult children pull away from her more and more in an effort to be independent and chart their own course.

Questions for Reflection

1. In what ways do you see the capacity of nurturing corrupted in your own life? When and how do you self-protect? When and how do you self-promote?

2. Name some situations when you either controlled or abdicated in your capacity to nurture.

3. When and in what ways do you struggle to nurture?

BIBLICAL PORTRAITS

NURTURING CORRUPTED: REBEKAH

READ GENESIS 24–27

At the start of Rebekah's story, she might appear to be a kindhearted and nurturing young woman. She provided nourishment to the servant and his camels, along with lodging for the night. She journeyed immediately to a foreign land and to a husband she had never met rather than staying with her family ten more days, and she comforted Isaac in the time of his mother's death. These are indicators of a kind, inviting, and nurturing young woman. Yet, the possibility of corrupting God-given capacities lies within each of us, and that is exactly what we see later in Rebekah's life.

After being barren for twenty years, Rebekah became pregnant. Curious as to why the baby jostled within her, Rebekah inquired of the Lord, who told her she would have twins and the older would serve the younger. That was counter-cultural in her time because the firstborn son was heir to the birthright. The birthright included the family name, titles, and inheritance of the family possessions. The traditional inheritance was not the only thing at stake here for Isaac's heir. Isaac's son, who would receive the birthright, would have a spiritual position in the covenant line of Abraham.

Scripture describes Esau, the elder of the twins, as brutish, hairy, and a skilled hunter who was always in the fields. It seems as though Esau did not think much of his spiritual heritage, impulsively and thoughtlessly selling his birthright as firstborn for a mere cup of stew. Esau even married outside of the Israelite people, taking two Hittite women as his wives, which made life bitter for Isaac and Rebekah (Genesis 26:35). On the opposite end of the spectrum, we see Jacob, a quiet man who always stayed close to home. We see favoritism in this family, as Genesis 25:28 tells us that Isaac loved Esau, but Rebekah loved Jacob.

Blind and nearing death, Isaac called Esau to him so that he could bless his son before he died. Rebekah overheard Isaac and devised a plan to ensure that Jacob received the blessing instead of Esau. She probably remembered the Lord's statement years earlier that the elder would serve the younger. But instead of inquiring of the Lord or discussing it with her husband, Rebekah acted autonomously. She ignored God, usurped her husband, and manipulated circumstances to bring about the outcome she thought best.

Our final glimpse into Rebekah's heart may be the most telling. Before Jacob fled to Laban, Rebekah said to her husband Isaac, "I loathe my life because of the Hittite women. If Jacob marries one of the Hittite women like these, one of the women of the land, what good will my life be to me?" (Genesis 27:46b ESV). It appears that Rebekah harbored bitterness toward her son Esau. Maybe she felt shamed by Esau's decision to marry Hittite women. Maybe she feared Esau's receiving the blessing, because he seemed to have so little regard for his spiritual heritage. Maybe she thought she knew what was best for her family. Whatever her motivation, Rebekah, rather than nurturing Esau and calling him to be a better man, despised him for his poor choices. Rather than creating a supportive environment, encouraging his development, or helping him become a better man, she condemned him.

Ultimately, Rebekah didn't trust God. She acted out of proud unbelief, and the consequences of her actions were far reaching. Strife and dissension between Jacob and Esau lasted for generations. Jacob had to flee to escape the murderous wrath of his brother. Both Isaac and Esau were deeply troubled by her deception. And, because she sent Jacob away to protect him from Esau, she died without ever seeing him again.

NURTURING REDEEMED: MARY OF BETHANY

READ MATTHEW 26:6–13, MARK 14:3–9, JOHN 12:1–8

The day of Jesus' death drew near. Jesus forewarned his disciples once again, "As you know, Passover begins in two days, and the Son of Man will be handed over to be crucified" (Matthew 26:2). These men, all of whom had been with Jesus during his three years of public ministry, had done everything from arguing among themselves over who would be first in the kingdom to rebuking Jesus when he spoke of his fate.

After three years of following him, listening to him, and being in intimate fellowship with him, they still didn't get it. They somehow seemed to miss all those times when Jesus told them the very reason he came was to die. Jesus, though fully God, was also fully man. He suffered in the flesh, feeling hunger, pain, loneliness, and sorrow just like we do. He knew the daunting task ahead of him; he felt the weight of the cross, yet his closest friends were oblivious. How lonely he must have felt!

Then, Mary of Bethany entered the scene as Jesus and his disciples gathered at Simon the leper's house for a feast. She broke open a flask of expensive perfume, amounting to around a year's wages, and poured it on Jesus' head and feet. With even more boldness, she unbound her hair, letting it fall around her shoulders, and she wiped Jesus' feet with it. It was a scandalous display. Not only had she let down her hair, which was regarded as sensual, but she had "wasted" perfume that could have been sold and given to the poor. The disciples scorned her for her foolishness. They still didn't get it.

But, Mary did. Her eyes were opened because she listened to Jesus, and she understood; she saw him. She recognized his need and she came alongside him. Through her unbridled display of humility, love, devotion, and nurture, Mary's actions whispered to Jesus, "Lord, I get it. I understand. I'm here to do all I can to help prepare you for what you must endure." Her act of nurturing provided encouragement and emboldened Jesus on his way to the cross. Jesus honored her, saying, "For she has done a beautiful thing to me . . . she has done it to prepare me for burial. Truly, I say to you, wherever this gospel is proclaimed in the whole world, what she has done will also be told in memory of her" (Matthew 26:10b, 12–13 ESV).

Questions for Reflection

1. What examples from the Bible or your own life illustrate positive ways to nurture?

2. What examples from the Bible or your own life illustrate negative ways to nurture?

05

PARTNERING

The last two chapters explored a woman's capacity to reflect the inviting and nurturing nature of God. In this chapter, we will explore the capacity of partnering within the *ezer* calling.

For the purpose of this study, we will define *partnering* as the intentional, proactive utilization of God-given gifts to bring strength and further a mutual cause. While nurturing builds up others to be who God desires them to be, partnering assists others in the movement toward a goal. Using her partnering capacity, a woman can advance the cause of another.

PARTNERING WITHIN THE TRINITY

THE MISSION OF CREATION

There is no better or more beautiful example of partnering than that of the Trinity. The relationship between God the Father, God the Son, and God the Holy Spirit is breathtaking: one God in three persons—each one equally God, yet different in function. From the very beginning, the partnership between each member is evident as they labored alongside one another in the mission of creation.

> In the beginning, ***God*** created the heavens and the earth. The earth was without form and void, and darkness was over the

> face of the deep. And the ***Spirit*** of God was hovering over the face of the waters.
>
> —Genesis 1:1–2 (ESV, emphasis added)

> ***Christ*** is the visible image of the invisible God. He existed before anything was created and is supreme over all creation, for through him God created everything in the heavenly realms and on earth. He made the things we can see and the things we can't see—such as thrones, kingdoms, rulers, and authorities in the unseen world. Everything was created through him and for him. He existed before anything else, and he holds all creation together.
>
> —Colossians 1:15–17 (emphasis added)

> But we know that there is only one God, the Father, who created everything, and we live for him. And there is only one Lord, Jesus Christ, through whom God made everything and through whom we have been given life.
>
> —1 Corinthians 8:6

PARTNERING WITHIN THE TRINITY

THE MISSION OF REDEMPTION

The Father, Son, and Holy Spirit each contributed to the mission of creation. Yet, their partnership doesn't end with creation. Scripture reveals that they continue to co-labor with one another in the redemption of the world. Each member of the Trinity is essential, making significant contributions in the life of a believer.

GOD THE FATHER

In John 3:16, we read that God loved the world so much that he gave his one and only Son, so that everyone who believes in him will not perish but have eternal life.

A holy God could have abandoned sinners to eternally suffer the consequences of their sin and rebellion. Yet, because of his great love for us, he sent his only Son to fulfill his plan of redemption. The Father granted Jesus authority over all people, and this authority was given so that he (Jesus) might give eternal life to all the Father had given him (John 17:2). God sent Jesus to die in our place as a fulfillment of the law, thereby providing us with a way to be reconciled to him for eternity.

JESUS

Jesus embodies the very essence of partnering. He came down from heaven not to do his own will but the will of the Father (John 6:38). Though he was despised and rejected by men, a man of sorrows, familiar with suffering, mocked, beaten, spat upon, and pierced for our transgressions, he did not waver in fulfilling the purpose for which he came. We see this determination in John 12:27 as he says, "Now my soul is deeply troubled. Should I pray, 'Father, save me from this hour'? But this is the very reason I came!" We see it most poignantly in the Garden of Gethsemane as he prays in agony and sweats drops of blood.

> "Father, if you are willing, please take this cup of suffering away from me. Yet I want your will to be done, not mine."
>
> —Luke 22:42

Jesus was so committed to the Father's mission that he "consciously, voluntarily, and obediently endured the cross."[17]

THE HOLY SPIRIT

In John chapter 16, Jesus reveals the importance of the Holy Spirit's role in the divine partnership.

> "But in fact, it is best for you that I go away, because if I don't, the Advocate won't come. If I do go away, then I will send him to you. And when he comes, he will convict the world of its sin, and of God's righteousness, and of the coming judgment . . . When the Spirit of truth comes, he will guide you into all truth. He will not speak on his own but will tell you what he has heard. He will tell you about the future."
>
> —John 16:7–8, 13

The Spirit guides us in truth, intercedes on our behalf, identifies us as children of God, and convicts us of sin. The Spirit owns the cause of the Father and Son, and furthers it through his sanctification work in the life of believers.

Partnering within the Trinity is evident throughout Scripture, as "each member of the Trinity speaks and acts in such a way as to enhance the reputations of the other two, to bring praise and honor to the other persons."[18] The Father, Son, and Holy Spirit co-labor equally, harmoniously, and sacrificially toward a shared mission.

But, what might this look like in the life of a woman? How can a woman utilize her strengths through partnering to assist another in moving toward a goal? Let's take a look at the life of one woman in Scripture who embodies the *ezer* calling through her capacity to invite, nurture, and partner.

Question for Reflection

1. Now that you see partnering within the Trinity, how does that affect the way you view partnering as a woman's core capacity?

THE WOMAN WOMEN LOVE TO HATE

PARTNERING AND THE PROVERBS 31 WOMAN

No other woman in Scripture has the ability to make women more frustrated than the Proverbs 31 woman. Her skills and abilities, her tenacity and influence have been hailed throughout the ages. Every woman who has measured herself against the Proverbs 31 woman feels she comes up short. However you may feel about this passage, the Proverbs 31 woman gives us an excellent example of partnering.

Whether married or single, with children or without, whether a stay-at-home mom or a woman in the workforce, whether crafty or sporty or none of the above, the Proverbs 31 woman is applicable to you as a woman. Rather than looking at her literally, let's take a step back and look at the transcendent principles behind her specific actions. What does the Proverbs 31 woman have to say about being a woman of noble character? How does she reflect the *ezer* calling and the capacities to invite, nurture, and partner?

> Who can find a virtuous and capable wife? She is more precious than rubies (v. 10).
>
> *She is valuable. She enriches the lives of others.*
>
> Her husband can trust her, and she will greatly enrich his life. She brings him good, not harm, all the days of her life (vs. 11–12).
>
> *She is trustworthy. She is loyal. She is someone who is for you.*
>
> She finds wool and flax and busily spins it. She is like a merchant's ship, bringing her food from afar (vs. 13–14).
>
> *She works diligently.*
>
> She gets up before dawn to prepare breakfast for her household and plan the day's work for her servant girls (v. 15).

She sacrifices, provides, and nurtures. She also leads and delegates.

She goes to inspect a field and buys it; with her earnings she plants a vineyard (v. 16).

She is discerning and resourceful. She is intelligent and capable.

She is energetic and strong, a hard worker.

She makes sure her dealings are profitable; her lamp burns late into the night. Her hands are busy spinning thread, her fingers twisting fiber (vs. 17–19).

She works hard. She is wise, shrewd, and a good steward of her time and resources.

She extends a helping hand to the poor and opens her arms to the needy (v. 20).

She is compassionate and serves others. She gives of what she has to those in need.

She has no fear of winter for her household, for everyone has warm clothes (v. 21).

She is intentional and prepared.

She makes her own bedspreads. She dresses in fine linen and purple gowns (v. 22).

She utilizes her skills and talents. She takes care of herself.

Her husband is well known at the city gates, where he sits with the other civic leaders (v. 23).

She contributes to the respect her husband receives and enables him to have a position of prominence.

She makes belted linen garments and sashes to sell to the merchants (v. 24).

> *She is resourceful and utilizes her talents and abilities.*
>
> She is clothed with strength and dignity, and she laughs without fear of the future (v. 25).
>
> *She is strong, whole, at rest, and at peace with herself because she entrusts herself to God.*
>
> When she speaks, her words are wise, and she gives instructions with kindness (v. 26).
>
> *She is engaged, discerning, wise, and kind in her interactions with others.*
>
> She carefully watches everything in her household and suffers nothing from laziness (v. 27).
>
> *She is an active participant and contributes relationally, emotionally, physically, and financially.*
>
> Her children stand and bless her. Her husband praises her: "There are many virtuous and capable women in the world, but you surpass them all!" (vs. 28–29).
>
> *Those who are in her life are blessed and better because she owns their causes, because she is for them.*
>
> Charm is deceptive, and beauty does not last; but a woman who fears the Lord will be greatly praised. Reward her for all she has done. Let her deeds publicly declare her praise (vs. 30–31).

Having looked at some of the transcendent attributes of this woman, let's look a little deeper at the passage and how it illustrates the feminine capacity of partnering. However, before we begin, one disclaimer is necessary. Because inviting, nurturing, and partnering are all interwoven within the feminine makeup, it is often hard to untangle the threads of inviting from those of nurturing or partnering. What is evident in the Proverbs 31 woman is that she is a woman who embodies the whole of the *ezer* calling. She brings all of who she is alongside those in her life in a way that is sacrificial, honoring, and beneficial to them.

In Proverbs 31, King Lemuel's mother is giving him advice on choosing a wife. This is wise counsel from a mother who has nurtured a son of royalty and now she partners with him in his mission to choose a suitable bride. This mother is being an essential counterpart in a way that enables her son to think wisely about his choice of the right partner for marriage. Not only is she helping her son but also an entire group of people within the kingdom as she gives recommendations for the qualities of the future queen. The ultimate goal of partnering is to advance the kingdom of God.

Partnering is active and intentional. The image of femininity within this passage is robust and without passivity. The woman described is strong and contributes relationally, emotionally, and financially. She knows herself and has cultivated skills. This woman knows what she is doing. She takes initiative to add income for the family, to help the poor, and to empower her husband. She is trustworthy. She initiates, plans, and strategizes. Because she has been a good steward of her resources, she operates out of excess.

She also offers herself as a resource, not just for her family but also for others. Her work has elevated her husband to a "man of substance" in their community. Her husband, as they age together, finds her more compelling and beautiful. Because this woman "fears the Lord," she lives obediently, with actions that are praiseworthy.

Partnering requires patience and steadfastness. The Proverbs 31 woman is a woman with a lifetime of work behind her. Many partnering relationships are lifelong connections. Rather than living and reacting in each moment, a woman who partners thinks strategically in terms of decades, not years.

This passage is not about being a seamstress, and to read it as such belittles what is being communicated. This portion of Scripture emphasizes a woman's virtue: her mercy, patience, ingenuity, self-understanding, and wisdom. Not all women must have the exact same talents, gifts, clothes, home decor, careers, education, and interests. A woman of virtue seeks to use her unique gifts and abilities to glorify God. The woman in Proverbs 31 knows herself and takes initiative to contribute based on who she is. Partnering is unique to your strengths and talents.

"When she speaks, her words are wise, and she gives instructions with kindness." **Partnering cannot be silent.** Constructive speech and instruction are necessary components of partnering. This type of speech is life giving and helpful. This is not a nibbling to death, constant dripping, or a quarrelsome communication style. So often, instruction becomes a way of pointing out the shortcomings of another person. But when instruction is given with discernment, wisdom, and kindness, it is life giving, subtle, and purposeful. How and *when* you say something is as important as *what* you say.

As with all gifts and talents entrusted to women by the Holy Spirit, wisdom is for the benefit of others. If wisdom is merely consumed and not exported, there is a problem. Seeking wisdom is not meant to be an end in itself. It should pierce, convict, and then compel others to go and do likewise. **Partnering requires wisdom.**

Sharing wisdom often requires discernment, humility, and vulnerability as you share from your own wounds, sins, and experiences. But when a woman entrusts her heart to Christ rather than withdrawing into self-protection, she is free to bare herself to another in a way that assists them in their mission.

As you think about partnering, you may feel overwhelmed at your inadequacies. It is important to remember that the partnering capacity is rooted in the principle of serving one another in love. When your heart is motivated by love, you are equipped to come alongside anyone in your life. **Partnering flows from a heart orientation of service.** But even in this, it is important to seek the Holy Spirit to transform self-protecting and self-promoting hearts toward others.

The Proverbs 31 woman may make you feel as if there is no way to measure up. But the purpose behind this portion of Scripture is not to provide an impossible "to do" list or to make you feel defeated. Because of your season of life or individuality, there are ways in which your life may not parallel the woman described. Rather than feeling marginalized by her, there is encouragement and inspiration to be found in the contribution a woman of God can make. Though this picture is an example of what a flourishing woman looks like in a particular time, culture, and season of life, her virtue is timeless. Your calling as an essential counterpart will be developed over time and in your own unique circumstance. God will bring it about in you as you make yourself available to him.

Questions for Reflection

1. How is the Proverbs 31 woman different from what you previously thought?

2. How does this passage affect your understanding of yourself as a woman?

3. The Proverbs 31 woman used her gifts, talents, and resources in a way that benefited those with whom she partnered. What gifts, talents, and resources do you have that could benefit those in your life? How could you partner with another in a way that furthers his or her cause?

PARTNERING IN THE LIFE OF A WOMAN

Woman was created with a unique mission: to further the advancement of another by contributing strength, support, assistance, and means. She is able to come alongside others and help shoulder their burdens.

> So God created man in his own image, in the image of God he created him; male and female he created them.
>
> —Genesis 1:27 (ESV)

> Then the LORD God said, "It is not good that the man should be alone; I will make him a *helper fit* (*ezer kenegdo*) for him."
>
> —Genesis 2:18 (ESV, emphasis added)

Though these two Genesis passages introduce us to partnering within marriage, the applications of this capacity are broad. Partnering extends not just to the relationship of a woman with her husband but also to her relationship with humanity in general. The applications of partnering reach beyond marital status. Partnering is not a role; it is a capacity. One may partner within marriage, but one need not be married to partner.

For example, a woman may have great organizational skills and an ability to rally people around a cause. Because of the unique talents she has, she partners with the director of a local nonprofit by organizing and facilitating a group of volunteers in a community enhancement project.

Another woman, though she is in a position of authority, may partner with her employees. Rather than using her employees to accomplish her goals and make herself look good, she utilizes her position to help them succeed in their projects. She invests time, energy, and money in them. And she is at work, behind the scenes, setting them up to succeed by freely sharing knowledge and resources available to her that can help further them in their careers.

Regardless of the application, it is important to understand that partnering is active and beneficial. Being an essential counterpart does not devalue a woman, nor does it mean she is of lesser value than the one with whom she aligns herself.

To understand and utilize the partnering capacity, there must be a transcendent vision that focuses strategically on using the gifts and talents God has entrusted to you.

In Romans 12:4–13, Paul exhorts believers as members of one body to "concentrate upon and give their energies to the gifts God has given them, whether in serving others, teaching God's Word patiently, or in exhortation and encouragement in the things of God."[19]

Later, in Romans 16:1–16, Paul commends several women, including those who have partnered with the church and with him in his mission to spread the good news of Jesus Christ among the Gentiles. Among those women, he names Phoebe, a woman who has clearly been a partner in Paul's life, as well as the lives of many others:

> I commend to you our sister Phoebe, who is a deacon in the church in Cenchrea. Welcome her in the Lord as one who is worthy of honor among God's people. Help her in whatever she needs, for she has been helpful to many, and especially to me.
>
> —Romans 16:1-2

This letter from Paul to the Romans is evidence of women partnering in many different ways, using their gifts to benefit the body of Christ. Based upon these two passages, we see that it is possible to partner with friends, coworkers, children, husbands, siblings, parents, mentors, coaches, leaders, and many other people. This will vary for each woman based on her season of life.

While we will address submission in the next section, it is important to note that, *partnering need not be limited to roles in which you are submitting*. There are times when you may be partnered as the authority figure. For example, a woman who serves alongside at-risk youth through tutoring is undoubtedly a type of authority in their lives, as their elder and as their tutor. Because she owns their mission to graduate, she brings her unique gifts and talents to bear in a way that propels them to succeed in school.

Again, partnering is a capacity that will be lived out differently according to your individuality and season of life. The applications are as varied as the individuals, but the goal is the same: to further another toward accomplishing a goal or cause through the intentional utilization of your strengths, talents, resources, and gifts.

Partnering is an orientation of the heart, a desire to join and serve another. As Paul taught, partnering includes thoughtful, vigorous resolve to come alongside and be an essential counterpart. It requires sacrifice, patience, and steadfastness. When a woman exercises her capacity to partner with others, she walks beside them as their ally or companion, as someone who sacrificially owns their causes. But what is the primary cause she is championing? Though there are many situational causes, there is one overarching cause: others were created in the image of God, and women are equipped to come alongside and ennoble them to reflect his image.

Questions for Reflection

1. How have you seen the capacity of partnering lived out well in another woman?

2. Considering your individuality and season, what are some relationships in which you are using your partnering capacity? How are you partnering in these relationships?

3. Describe an example of partnering you have experienced or witnessed in the past week.

4. What other examples of partnering do you see in Romans 16:1–16?

THE DREADED "S" WORD

THE ROLE OF SUBMISSION IN PARTNERING

The Proverbs 31 woman and submission encompass two of the most heated topics among women in today's Christian culture. People on both sides of the debate, ranging from staunch feminists to extreme fundamentalists, typically have an incomplete or inaccurate understanding of submission. In general, submission is the voluntary humbling of oneself in order to elevate another. Regardless of season or life circumstances, whether you are single or married, submission is relevant to who you are as a woman.

Submission is only one aspect of partnering. Submission was part of Christ partnering with the Father (Luke 22:42). Even in equality, there is submission. Though Jesus is equal in divinity and power, he willfully humbles himself and elevates the Father through the act of submission. Just as Christ submits to the Father, submission is part of a woman's calling to be an essential counterpart.

Submission is a divine attribute. Jesus Christ is eternally submitted to God the Father, and he does not feel devalued by that. He is not a lesser, unequal part of the Trinity. He is valuable and significant. The Father's plan would not have been fulfilled had Christ not submitted. He chose to submit. As image-bearers, women have the honor of reflecting Christ's submission in partnering.

There are misconceptions within our culture of what it means to be submissive. Society tends to view submission as compliance, subservience, passivity, or weakness, but that is not biblical submission. Submission is not a last resort of giving up when two people just can't agree. True submission includes a free exchange of ideas. There is a mutual respect for one another's opinions and skills. Within submission, there is healthy interdependence.

Culture often equates position with value, but this is simply not biblical. Although position differs, value remains the same. It is not an issue of equality or value; it is an issue of honor and respect. Someone must submit in order for another to lead. Knowing this enables a woman to read Ephesians 5:21–33 without fear of being degraded. And further, to submit to her husband out of reverence for Christ.

> For wives, this means submit to your husbands as to the Lord. For a husband is the head of his wife as Christ is the head of the church. He is the Savior of his body, the church. As the

> church submits to Christ, so you wives should submit to your husbands in everything.
>
> For husbands, this means love your wives, just as Christ loved the church. He gave up his life for her to make her holy and clean, washed by the cleansing of God's Word. He did this to present her to himself as a glorious church without a spot or wrinkle or any other blemish. Instead, she will be holy and without fault. In the same way, husbands ought to love their wives as they love their own bodies. For a man who loves his wife actually shows love for himself. No one hates his own body but feeds and cares for it, just as Christ cares for the church. And we are members of his body.
>
> As the Scriptures say, "A man leaves his father and mother and is joined to his wife, and the two are united into one." This is a great mystery, but it is an illustration of the way Christ and the church are one. So again I say, each man must love his wife as he loves himself, and the wife must respect her husband.
>
> —Ephesians 5:22–33

Submission to a husband is an aspect of partnering within the marital relationship. It is sacrificial and requires a heart orientation of being on the same team. As a wife follows the leadership of her husband, there are benefits, but there are also difficulties. A woman's security cannot be found in her marriage relationship. She is secure because she trusts God.

As partners, there is a responsibility to speak truth to one another in love. This may include rebuke. For a wife, withholding truth and insight from her husband is not submission; that is despising him. Husbands and wives can disagree, but what needs to undergird everything is that they are on the same team. A wife who submits to her husband respectfully acknowledges the responsibility he carries, and she bears and shares the risk with him.

Submission is knowing with whom you will partner and willingly placing yourself under their leadership. Biblical submission in disagreement involves sharing your insight and wisdom and then assuring your partner that, though you may not agree, you will follow, except when to do so would lead you both into sin.

Owning the cause of another requires determination, strength, and wisdom. Submission is not begrudging. It is not a position that says, "I'll do whatever you say no matter how wrong it may be." Rather, it is a position that says, "I want you to succeed. I'm with you. I will push behind your cause. I want you to follow Christ in your calling, and I will sacrifice for that purpose." In her submission, she enables her husband to lead because she is following, and through her submission, she intentionally owns his cause.

WHAT ABOUT SINGLES?

So what about the single woman? Are there any universal principles of submission that apply to all women, regardless of marital status?

There are many passages in Scripture regarding submission of all believers. James calls all believers to submit to God (James 4:7). In Romans 13:1–5, Paul addresses the importance of submission to governing authorities. First Peter 5:5 urges younger people to submit to their elders. The author of the book of Hebrews calls believers to obey their leaders and submit to their authority because "they keep watch over you as men who must give an account" (Hebrews 13:17). And Ephesians 5:21 calls all believers to submit to one another out of reverence for Christ. In all of these passages, it is evident that the heart of biblical submission is reverence for Christ and love and respect for one another.

Regardless of your marital status, submission is an act of obedience for all Christians. It is one that requires us to humble ourselves and elevate others. Every woman can submit, but submission to authority is not the same as submission to a husband. This is where we must bring clarity to many younger women who mistakenly believe that because they are women, they must submit to all men. But this is simply not biblical. For example, consider a young woman who is partnered with several young men for a group project. Just because her teammates are men does not mean they are her authority and that she must submit to their direction. In fact, in some situations, it would be entirely appropriate for her to take a leadership role, providing direction and oversight to the team. In this way, she exercises her partnering capacity with the group toward a shared goal. However, as a woman who follows Christ, her call is still to honor and respect those on her team and to bring her strengths to bear in a way that furthers the cause of her team, not herself. And this flows from a deep, personal reverence for Christ.

Nevertheless, there are some transcendent principles of submission that can honor the Lord in every woman's calling as an *ezer*. By placing herself under the authority of another, she rejects autonomy. Many single, adult women function throughout their day-to-day lives in complete autonomy. Because she is no longer under her parents' authority, she operates in a silo—making all of her own decisions—doing what she wants, whenever and however she wants. To be certain, this is good and part of growing up. However, all of us need the wisdom, direction, and insight of others speaking into our lives. We all need someone to hold us accountable and, at times, to operate as an authority in our lives. Single women can reject autonomy by willingly placing godly authority in their lives through mentor relationships, pastors, accountability couples, teachers, small group leaders, and even friends. By submitting to another, you willingly humble yourself, admitting that you do not always know what is best.

In partnering relationships in which one is paired with authority, submission is not blind and thoughtless following, but more of a thoughtful, intentional deferring to another's judgment, opinion, or decision. This requires humility and openness to the ideas and direction of others. A submissive spirit is flexible, respectful, accommodating, and quick to see where others may be right. Submission is not always easy. In fact, in many cases it is sacrificial; it requires dying to self and relinquishing your own desire to be right or to be in control. But the fruit of biblical submission is order, harmony, and peace;

whereas chaos, division, strife, disunity, and individualism reign when we are unwilling to submit to the authorities God places in our lives.

Ultimately, submission is first and foremost to God, and the evidence of submission to God will be manifested through the act of submission to other authorities in our lives.

Questions for Reflection

1. In what ways is a biblical understanding of submission different from your previous thoughts about it?

2. How does submission exhibit strength rather than weakness or passivity?

3. How does knowing that Jesus is eternally submitted to the Father change how you feel about submission?

4. Describe how submission might benefit the person to whom you submit. How do you benefit from submitting?

5. What struggles do you have in submitting?

HOW DOES AUTONOMY CORRUPT PARTNERING?

As we have discussed, partnering is the intentional, proactive utilization of God-given gifts to bring strength and further the cause of another. However, because of a woman's temptation toward autonomy, self becomes her main objective.

In Matthew 25:14–28, Jesus tells a parable about three servants and their master. Before the master leaves town, he entrusts each servant with a portion of talents to steward while he is away. When the master comes home, two of the servants double the return to him because they invested the talents given to them. The third servant, however, buried his talent and returns to his master only the original gift. The master praises his first two servants for being good stewards of what had been given to them, but he chastises the third servant for not investing what had been given to him.

Like the servants, God has entrusted women with gifts and talents. A woman's giftings are not her own; they belong to God. When a woman invests these divine giftings in others, she advances the kingdom of God. However, when she buries the talents or hoards them for the advancement of her own kingdom, she rejects God's ultimate authority and ownership. This is autonomy. She may withdraw in self-protection and reject her calling to utilize her gifts to assist another, or in self-promotion, she may leverage her gifts to advance her own cause. Either is a corruption of her God-given gifts.

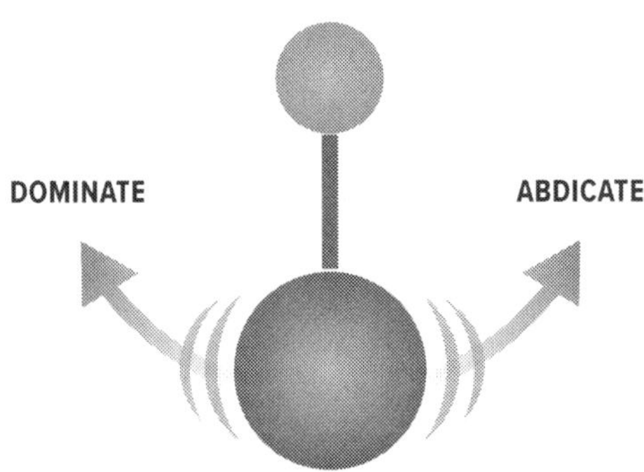

At times, women tend to abdicate their responsibilities as partners. At other times, they may lean toward domineering in an attempt to govern or control. When you move away from partnering in relationships, your responses can fluctuate anywhere on this pendulum. Both sides are expressions of a refusal to partner. Whether you disown or control, it's an expression of the belief that your cause, your happiness, your comfort, or your mission is more important than another's. But just as we have stated, the goal is not a perfect halfway point between the two poles. The idea is not to try to limit controlling behavior or take more ownership; to truly partner means to break away from the pendulum. Through the power of the gospel, you can break free; you do not have to ride the pendulum. As Christ partnered to glorify the Father, women also can advance a mutual cause to glorify Christ.

Following are a few ways in which the capacity to partner may be corrupted.

A WOMAN WHO . . .

A woman who elevates her position in the workplace. Without her constant intervention, she believes the organization would suffer. She always feels the need to fix what her boss messes up. She does not own the cause of her supervisor, working in a way that honors him. Rather, she promotes herself by communicating the shortcomings of her boss to anyone who will listen. In her gossip, she is not benefiting her authority or the organization. She is actually finding value by feeling superior to the person with whom she should be partnering.

A woman who finds her identity in her mothering role. She finds it difficult to move from nurturing to partnering. Here, failure to launch meets failure to partner. Since her value is in being a "good mom," she feels she will lose something by letting go of her mommy role. Instead of partnering, she wants to keep things in her realm of control. Most likely, her actions will cause her children to react negatively. Instead of coming to her for wisdom and counsel, her children will feel the need to break away from her for freedom.

A woman who appears to have the submission idea down to a science. She is happy to go along for the ride as long as she can stay comfortable. She perceives herself as having a gentle and quiet spirit when in fact she is passive in her capacity as a partner. Failing to lend strength, she avoids conflict with her husband at all costs. She believes she is submitting, but rather than bringing strength to her husband in a way that helps him and eases his burden, she is abdicating and increasing his burden instead.

A woman who won't partner because she is afraid that someone else will interfere with her dreams. She knows the direction she wants to go in life and does not want to be restrained or disappointed. Because her idol is security, she fears the sacrifices partnering may require.

A woman who, in her relationship with someone (e.g. boss, husband, child, coworker, project lead), believes that person is making the wrong decision. She either disregards the other person's decision and makes her own, or she hides behind that person and blames him or her when things don't go the way she wants. Her thinking is, "I'll do what you say, even though I think this is a stupid choice. It's not my fault if it fails."

A woman whose need for affirmation drives her to alter her behavior to please the person to whom she's relating at any given moment. She puts up a front to feel socially acceptable. She has the right answers in her small group discussions at church, but no one really knows her true thoughts. Because she cares so much about what others think of her, she is not honest about her struggles; she fears being judged. When she could be partnering with others for growth, she is missing opportunity because of her fear of rejection and her need to look good.

A woman who pretends to be willing to partner because it makes her look good. She may allow others to do the work, but she manipulates behind the scenes to control the outcome or to take credit. She may superficially agree to partner then refuse to do anything to further the cause. This woman is concerned with how things look on the outside, but she is not actually willing to do the hard work required. She never addresses the heart issues of control and need for recognition with which she struggles.

A woman who is willing to partner only with causes that she approves of, agrees with, or likes. She is not willing to take any risk but instead promotes her own agenda through subtle manipulation, nagging, and emotional bullying. She may at times go along begrudgingly but is quick to remind others of their past failures and what all she is risking by following them.

A woman who has very low self-esteem. She is worried that her ideas are not valid or worthwhile and that she has nothing to offer. Her fear of rejection keeps her from using her God-given gifts to partner. Her self-protection keeps her focus on herself, and she is not free to reach out to others in her life.

A woman who cannot accept someone else's leadership. She always has to be in charge. She considers herself to be a natural leader, and she is not willing to submit to the authority of anyone, especially a man, because she does not believe they can lead as well as she can.

A woman who remains detached and doesn't want to get involved in another's cause. It's just easier for her to stay out of it because getting involved is too complicated. In her self-protection, she never steps up to share responsibility.

A woman who is overly competitive and believes that she can "have it all." She doesn't understand other women who can't accomplish as much as she can. She wants to win and always has to have the last word. She never admits that she's wrong or confesses any weakness.

Her self-promotion blinds her to her arrogant attitude and keeps her from recognizing when and where she is called to partner. She thinks she has it all under control on her own; she doesn't need help, and she can't understand why others think they do.

Just as the Holy Spirit is your advocate and your helper, you are an advocate for those around you. Partnering is hard work; it requires a heart for God and a heart for others. But he that has called you is faithful and will do it (1 Thessalonians 5:24).

In the next chapter, we will explore how the gospel is the power that frees women from the continuum of self-protection and self-promotion.

Questions for Reflection

1. In what ways have you corrupted partnering? Where have you rejected authority in your life? Where have you been passive in partnering?

2. When do you tend to abdicate responsibility and fail to partner? When do you tend to try to control rather than partner?

3. Describe an example of corrupt partnering that you have committed, experienced, or witnessed in the past week.

BIBLICAL PORTRAITS

A PORTRAIT OF SELF-PROMOTION: SAPPHIRA

READ ACTS 5:1–11

> All the believers were united in heart and mind. And they felt that what they owned was not their own, so they shared everything they had . . . There were no needy people among them, because those who owned land or houses would sell them and bring the money to the apostles to give to those in need.
>
> —Acts 4:32, 34–35

The church was small, but it was growing steadily. All the believers were together and held everything in common. The rich provided for the poor; no one was needy or hungry. What we see among the members of the early church is unity, fellowship, selflessness, and brotherly love. Each individual voluntarily did his or her part to care for the whole. And each day, the Lord added to their fellowship those who were being saved (Acts 2:47).

But one man among them, named Ananias, held wickedness in his heart. Ananias decided to sell a piece of property and pretentiously give the proceeds to the church. With Sapphira's full consent, Ananias secretly withheld a portion for himself. Ananias piously laid the money at Peter's feet, deceptively allowing others to believe that he had given the full amount of his sale. Peter exposed Ananias's deceit, and Ananias immediately fell dead. Three hours later, Peter questioned Sapphira, giving her an opportunity to tell the truth. But she also lied about the money, and she too dropped dead.

From Peter's questioning, we surmise that Ananias and Sapphira were not required to sell what they had or to give all of the proceeds to the church. Both the land and the profits from its sale were theirs to do with as they saw fit. Their sin was not necessarily in keeping some of the profit for themselves. It was instead in attempting to promote or elevate themselves through deception. This was not an act of faith. Motives were not rooted in the glory of God and the good of the church. Instead, they acted out of proud unbelief and selfishness, seeking their own public recognition and good standing among their peers.

What can we learn about partnering from Sapphira? Could it be that her desire for self-promotion motivated her to partner with Ananias in sin—or could her desire for self-protection have caused her to shrink back and abdicate her responsibility as his partner? Whatever took place in Sapphira's heart and mind, we know this to be true: she partnered with her husband in sin, and it resulted in both of their deaths.

As women, God has called us to own the cause of another, to be on the side of another, to love and serve another, and to speak truth to another, not just blindly agree. Abdication or leaving another to fend for his or herself is not partnering. God has granted women wisdom and insight, giving them the responsibility to use it for the good of the others and for the good of the church. Respectfully speaking truth or rebuking another is not in opposition to partnering or submission but is, in fact, part of it. In the case of Ananias and Sapphira, because he was bent on sin, she would have been well within her bounds to go to Peter, if she had first appealed to Ananias.

Though Sapphira was not responsible for Ananias's foolish choice, she was responsible for hers. She chose not to speak truth to Ananias. She chose to join him in sin rather than owning his cause and calling him to live in the light of truth. She failed to lend strength to help him live as the man God created him to be. She aided her husband in his foolishness and his ultimate destruction.

Ironically, Sapphira's name means "beautiful," but the legacy she left behind was far from beautiful. It was, instead, one of deceit, pride, hypocrisy, and ultimately death.

PARTNERING REDEEMED: RAHAB

READ JOSHUA 2 AND JOSHUA 6 (SEE ALSO MATTHEW 1:5, JAMES

2:25, AND HEBREWS 11:31)

> You are the LORD, you alone. You have made heaven, the heaven of heavens, with all their host, the earth and all that is on it, the seas and all that is in them; and you preserve all of them; and the host of heaven worships you. You are the LORD, the God who chose Abram and brought him out of Ur of the Chaldeans and gave him the name Abraham. You found his heart faithful before you, and made with him the covenant to give to his offspring the land of the Canaanite, the Hittite, the Amorite, the Perizzite, the Jebusite, and the Girgashite. And you have kept your promise, for you are righteous. And you saw the affliction of our fathers in Egypt and heard their cry at the Red Sea, and performed signs and wonders against Pharaoh and all his servants and all the people of his land, for you knew that they acted arrogantly against our fathers. And you made a name for yourself, as it is to this day. And you divided the sea before them, so that they went through the midst of the sea on dry land, and you cast their pursuers into the depths, as a stone into mighty waters. By a pillar of cloud you led them in the day, and by a pillar of fire in the night to light for them the way in which they should go.
>
> —Nehemiah 9:6–12 (ESV)

The above passage sets the stage for us as we peer into the life of a Canaanite woman named Rahab, a prostitute who inhabited the land of Jericho. For forty years, the Israelites wandered in the desert outside the land of Canaan. For forty years, the name and renown of the God of the Israelite people struck terror in the hearts of their enemies. For forty years, the stories of his mighty deeds spread throughout the land.

The God of Israel was the God who swallowed up his children's pursuers in the Red Sea. He led them in a pillar of cloud by day and fire by night; he protected them and delivered their enemies into their hands. He performed many signs and wonders and sustained his people in the desert for forty years. Imagine the fear of the people of Jericho as they realized the same God was camped just outside of their land on the other side of the Jordan with the Israelite people.

As Joshua prepared to lead the Israelites into the Promised Land, he sent two spies to scout out the territory. Upon coming into the city, the men found lodging in the house of a prostitute named Rahab. After hiding the spies and sending the king of Jericho on a bogus pursuit, Rahab boldly declared her faith in Yahweh to the Israelite spies,

> "I know that the LORD has given you the land, and that the fear of you has fallen upon us, and that all the inhabitants of the land melt away before you. For we have heard how the LORD dried up the water of the Red Sea before you when you came out of Egypt, and what you did to the two kings of the Amorites who were beyond the Jordan, to Sihon and Og, whom you devoted to destruction. And as soon as we heard it, our hearts melted, and there was no spirit left in any man because of you, for the LORD your God, he is God in the heavens above and on the earth beneath."
>
> —Joshua 2:9–11 (ESV)

Though she was a Gentile prostitute living in a wicked land, she'd heard the stories of Yahweh's power, might, and faithfulness. He wasn't like the idols her people worshiped. Rahab saw something different about the God of Israel. She believed him to be the one true God, the God who commands the heavens and the earth. Surely she was afraid of what would become of Jericho and its inhabitants at the hands of this God. Surely she was afraid of what might become of her and her family. But fear didn't stop her. She was willing to risk her own life to partner with God and the Israelite people.

When the spies showed up at her front door, Rahab seized the opportunity. She was intentional and directional. She not only hid the spies from the king of Jericho but also provided them with wisdom, insight, and direction on how to flee Jericho safely. Before they left the city, however, she secured her own safety, as well as the safety of her entire family.

Her willingness to bear and share the risk enabled the Israelite spies to have a successful mission and played an active part in furthering God's covenant promise to Abraham.

Rahab acted boldly on behalf of Yahweh, the Israelites, and her own family. Because of her strength, boldness, and faith in action, she and her family were spared when the walls of Jericho fell. Her family was protected by Israel, but her story doesn't end there. We see later in Scripture that Rahab eventually dwelt among the Israelites. Rahab became the mother of Boaz, the father of Obed, the father of Jesse, the father of King David, who is the line of the Messiah. God redeemed Rahab's life because of her belief, giving this former pagan prostitute a place of honor in the lineage of Christ and heralding her as one of the heroes of faith (Hebrews 11:5).

Questions for Reflection

1. What examples from the Bible or your own life illustrate positive ways to partner?

2. What examples from the Bible or your own life illustrate negative ways to partner?

06

THE GOSPEL TRUTH

Over the last five chapters, we've explored what it means to be an image-bearer. We have looked at a woman's core calling as an essential counterpart and her core temptation to be autonomous. We have also explored the three core capacities of inviting, nurturing, and partnering and the various ways in which women display these capacities in corrupted and redeemed ways. For many of you, the reality of your sin has come into clear view as you have worked through the material.

Some of you may have discovered your tendencies toward self-promotion in dating relationships, at work, in your marriages, or even among your friends. Maybe you are looking back on wreckage brought on by years of self-protection. Some of you may have discovered years of idolizing your children and unhealthy nurturing. Perhaps you feel you have more clarity about what it means to be a woman created in the image of God and how to live that out on a daily basis.

As you wrestle with this new knowledge of yourself, you may be tempted to manage your sin and circumstances. The reality of your sin may frustrate you and tempt you to despair. You may even try to fix yourself—or maybe you will strive to be more inviting, nurturing, and partnering and find yourself wearied by your efforts. It is important to note that if you are not careful, these attempts become nothing more than "holy autonomy" or an attempt to "right yourself" on your own terms.

While it is right to feel sorrowful over sin and to strive to be holy, these things must be rooted in the truth of the gospel. The desire to live a perfect, sin-free life can be a symptom of pride and just one more way we strive to live independent of Jesus.

In his article, "The Centrality of the Gospel," Tim Keller says:

> "Though religious persons may be extremely penitent and sorry for their sins, they see sins as simply the failure to live up to standards by which they are saving themselves. They do not see sin as the deeper self-righteousness and self-centeredness through which they are trying to live lives independent of God. So when they go to Jesus for forgiveness, they go only as a way to 'cover over the gaps' in their project of self salvation."[20]

If this is you, if you are your own biggest project, constantly striving to reach that place where you never mess up, then the gospel offers you peace and rest through the finished work of Christ on the cross and the promised sanctifying work of the Holy Spirit.

The struggle with sin is still very real on this side of heaven. You are an image-bearer, and you are a sinner. Because of sin, your ability to perfectly reflect God's image is broken. But, everything that was broken in the garden, including your ability to reflect his image, has been and is being restored through Jesus.

Whatever you may feel, whatever your struggle or circumstance, you will not be able to manage this on your own. You may be able to modify your behavior for a while, but it will not be sustainable apart from the hope and power of the gospel. "We are not just justified (saved) by the gospel and then sanctified (changed, made holy) by obedience. The gospel is the way we grow (Galatians 3:1–3) and are renewed (Colossians 1:6) . . . Both confession and 'hard work' that is not arising from and 'in line' with the gospel will not sanctify you—it will strangle you."[21]

THE GOSPEL TRUTH IS THIS:

Though you were once alienated from God and considered his enemy because of your sin, God reconciled you to himself through Christ's death on the cross (Colossians 1:21–23). Christ suffered the weight of your sin; he bore the punishment you deserved. Because of Christ's death in your place, God forgave all your sin, canceling the written code (the law) that condemned you, nailing it to the cross (Colossians 2:13–14). And by that one offering, he forever *made perfect* those who *are being made holy* (Hebrews 10:14).

God transferred Jesus' status to you, declaring you righteous and justified. You stand before God, not just as one who never sinned, but as one who has fulfilled his law in every way. The result of all this is that you have been released from slavery to sin and death. Though you are still a sinner and will continue to sin on this side of heaven, you are declared righteous, holy, and blameless. Though you were an enemy of God, you are now reconciled to him. Though you were once alienated, you have been brought into the family of God.

> But when the right time came, God sent his Son, born of a woman, subject to the law. God sent him to buy freedom for us who were slaves to the law, so that he could adopt us as his very own children. And because we are his children, God has sent the Spirit of his Son into our hearts, prompting us to call out, "Abba, Father." Now you are no longer a slave but God's own child. And since you are his child, God has made you his heir.
>
> —Galatians 4:4–7

You do not live as one who has no hope. You do not live as one who has no future. You are no longer utterly helpless or without resources or power. You have not been abandoned, orphaned, or left to fend for yourself. God decided in advance to adopt you into his own family by bringing you to himself through Jesus Christ. This is what he wanted to do, and it gave him great pleasure (Ephesians 1:5). You are no longer an orphan; you are a daughter. And because you are a daughter, he has also made you an heir (Galatians 4:7).

The Creator of the universe became your Father. He claims you, clothes you in his righteousness, and provides for you in this life and in the life to come. Your status as a daughter and an heir was secured through Jesus' blood alone, not because of anything you have done or will do. As an heir, you can now live with great expectation and hope because you "have a priceless inheritance—an inheritance that is kept in heaven for you, pure and undefiled, beyond the reach of change and decay. And through your faith, God is protecting you by his power until you receive this salvation, which is ready to be revealed on the last day for all to see" (1 Peter 1:4–5).

> [God] has identified us as his own by placing the Holy Spirit in our hearts as the first installment that guarantees everything he has promised us.
>
> —2 Corinthians 1:22

As a daughter and an heir, God has entrusted you with his Spirit as a guarantee of your future inheritance. The same Spirit that raised Jesus from the dead now lives in you, identifies you as a daughter of the King, and gives you everything you need for living a godly life (2 Peter 1:3–4). This is the truth of the gospel, and it is, indeed, very good news.

Questions for Reflection

1. As this study has revealed your sin, what temptations have you wrestled with?

2. What parts of the gospel truth presented in this section do you struggle to believe?

3. Do you think of God as your Father? How does your family of origin affect how you understand God as Father?

4. What does it mean to be orphaned? What challenges do orphans face? How do you relate to these challenges?

5. Describe the significance of adoption to an orphan. How does this affect how you view your own spiritual adoption?

LIVING LIKE AN ORPHAN

Maybe you are thinking, "This all sounds good, but how does this help me in my struggle with autonomy? How does this free me from self-protection and self-promotion? I need something more tangible, more practical."

This is a legitimate concern that we do not wish to minimize in any way. However, we want to stress that the gospel that saved you is the same gospel that changes you. All too often, women do not live in the good news of the gospel. Rather, they strive through their own efforts and resources to affect lasting change in their own lives. And the result is weary, powerless, burdened, and jaded believers. They live as orphans instead of daughters.

But this is not what Jesus means when he says, "Take my yoke upon you" (Matthew 11:29). Jesus' yoke is easy, and his burden is light (v. 30). In his commentary on this passage, Matthew Henry says Christ does have "a yoke for our necks," but that he also has a "crown for our heads." He continues by saying to take Christ's yoke upon us is to make ourselves servants to and subjects of him, and then to conduct ourselves in "conscientious obedience to all his commands, and a cheerful submission to all his disposals: it is to obey the gospel of Christ, to yield ourselves to the Lord."[22]

The gospel of Christ leads to life, power, and rest. All of his commandments are holy, just, and good. It is sin in us that makes them burdensome. Jesus' yoke is "lined with love," and it is "not only easy, it is also gracious, sweet, and pleasant . . . the love of God and the hope of heaven make it easy."[23]

So, how can a woman tell if she is living as an orphan or a daughter? The fruit of her life is often a good indicator.

A woman who thinks like an orphan is embittered when things don't happen according to her plan. She is often irritable, restless, and discontent. She is, at times, frustrated with the Lord for not granting her the desires of her heart, and she feels entitled to more from life than she's been given. As a result, she often has trouble feeling joy for others' successes or good fortunes.

A woman who thinks like an orphan is driven by fear and a need to control or manage the people and circumstances of her life, and she is frustrated when others don't cooperate. She needs assurances, security, and promise of a pain-free life. She struggles to protect herself from anything that could derail her plan.

A woman who thinks like an orphan is unwilling to have others speak into her life, challenge her choices, or provide her with direction. She has determined her course. Her heart is captured and driven by her own desires, goals, plans, and dreams. She considers herself the sole authority in her life. Her agenda drives her to promote herself and her needs above all others.

A woman who thinks like an orphan finds life and identity in her roles and circumstances. Because she has no transcendent direction, purpose, or mission, she is lost and confused. She is cynical because life, friends, men, and God continue to let her down. She feels hopeless and resigned to life.

A woman who thinks like an orphan is enslaved to her idols of family, marriage, approval, comfort, security, affirmation, success, beauty, or love. She is dependent upon these things for fulfillment, assurance, identity, and hope. But, ultimately, the idol underneath all of her other idols is that of self. She is trying to create her own kingdom where she rules and reigns, rather than living as daughter of the King and servant in his kingdom.

A woman who thinks like an orphan is weary from all her striving. Always seeking to "get it right" and frustrated when she falls short of her self-imposed standard once again. She works hard to be "pleasing to the Lord" or to "be a good Christian." But because she believes his pleasure is based on her own performance, she is worn out and despairing.

At first glance, "orphan" traits may sound easy to identify. Perhaps you've ruled yourself out. But the orphan mentality is often an insidious, silent killer. It can even be cloaked in good deeds, noble causes, or religion. The ways in which you think like an orphan are as varied as each woman. Identifying your orphan tendencies will require earnest seeking, reflection, prayer, and transparency in authentic relationships. The end result of turning from this mentality is freedom and true life.

TRAITS OF AN ORPHAN

FEAR/CONTROL

When you are afraid and your tendency is to try to manage and control life, what is the lie that you are choosing to believe? More often than not, fear is a case of misplaced hope. Fear results when you believe that your hope is based in your ability to control your circumstances. You may fear losing a loved one, never getting married, not getting your dream job, losing the love of your spouse, being rejected, failure, or never having assurance of your child's salvation. Ultimately, you have not placed your hope in God but in your ability to manage and control life to suit you.

Your fear and misplaced hope needs to be redirected to a God who reigns sovereign over everything—including your deepest fears. Jesus endured the cross by faith in the hope of the future joy set before him. He placed his hope solely on the perfect, good, loving, and holy will of the Father. Because his hope was in God alone, Jesus was able to trust God even in rejection, betrayal, abandonment, suffering, and death. Jesus believed in the truth of God's character and his word.

This does not mean that Jesus cannot identify with you in your fear. On the contrary, in the garden, before his arrest and crucifixion, Jesus was overwhelmed at what was to come. He prayed three times that the Lord would provide another way (Matthew 26:36–46). But, he did not move into a position of self-protection. He trusted God and followed him—scorned, rejected, and mocked—all the way to the cross.

Because of Jesus' example, because of the truth of a faithful, powerful God who is your *Ezer* and who is for you, you can move out of the bondage of self-protection and self-promotion. You can endure life circumstances that seem out of control and scary, entrusting yourself to your Creator and reflecting his image in spite of uncertainty and disappointment.

GUILT

When you are burdened by guilt over your past sins, what is the lie you are choosing to believe? More often than not, guilt is a problem of misplaced faith, of unbelief. Guilt is focused on your own behavior, your performance and failures. Prolonged guilt comes from believing that Jesus' performance is not enough to cover you and that you need to perform in order to pay for your sins. Guilt is a vicious taskmaster, robbing you of all the freedom that is yours in Christ. When you feel you have performed well, you swing toward pride. When you feel you have performed poorly, you swing toward despair. Neither response is based in the truth and power of the gospel to save and change you. If you feel close to God when you are doing well and far from God when you fail, you do not fully believe or understand the gospel. Rather, you believe in yourself as your own functional savior.

Why did Jesus humble himself, taking on flesh in order to live a perfect life and die a painful death on the cross if all it takes is your guilt-powered performance to save you and affect change in your life?

Guilt and conviction are a natural response to sin. But, if guilt remains focused on self rather than driving you toward godly sorrow (2 Corinthians 7:10), you will move into self-protection or self-promotion as you try to prove yourself to God and others. When you redirect your misplaced faith to Christ, trusting in him as your Savior, you are declared justified—just as if you never sinned. Not only does God declare you not guilty, but he also declares you holy, without blemish, and without accusation (Colossians 1:21–23). It is not your performance that counts before God; it is Christ's performance alone. God placed your record of sin and failure upon Christ, and he placed Christ's perfect obedience upon you.

Claiming the truth of the gospel is a moment-by-moment process. As fallen beings, "we are not near as vigorous in appropriating God's forgiveness as he is in extending it."[24] Will you always have it together? Will your motives always be pure? Not on this side of heaven. However, when you stand firm in the truth of your status before God, you are freed from your guilt. Moving forward in this freedom, you are able to more fully reflect his image through inviting, nurturing, and partnering.

SHAME

When you are ashamed, what is the lie you are choosing to believe? Shame is a fear of being exposed in your weakness. Shame comes from believing the lie that your identity, who you are, is based on how you or others perceive you. Shame is different from guilt. Guilt says, "I *made* a mistake; I *did* something bad," but shame says, "I *am* a mistake; I *am* bad."[25] Where guilt is focused on behavior, shame is focused on self. It is rooted in the belief that you are not good enough. Therefore, you are driven by a desire to cover your weaknesses and failings. To expose yourself, to be vulnerable and allow another to know you fully, is too much of a threat. And so, you move into self-protection, never allowing yourself to be fully known—or you move into self-promotion, attempting to overcompensate for your weaknesses.

In your unwillingness to be vulnerable with others, you are never free to fully love another or be loved by another. When freedom is available to you, you choose to remain enslaved to your need to maintain an acceptable identity. You work hard to keep up appearances and keep people at a safe distance. You are not living in the truth and freedom of the gospel.

The gospel says that, "God sent his Son, born of a woman, subject to the law. God sent him to buy freedom for us who were slaves to the law, so that he could adopt us as his very own children. And because we are his children, God has sent the Spirit of his Son into our hearts, prompting us to call out, 'Abba, Father.' Now you are no longer a slave but God's own child. And since you are his child, God has made you his heir" (Galatians 4:4b–6).

In the beginning, God created a world in which there was *no shame* (Genesis 2:25). When sin entered the world, shame followed on its coattails. But Jesus, because of the joy awaiting him, endured the cross and *despised its shame* (Hebrews 12:2). Christ bore your shame on the cross, so that you might be adopted into the family of God. Because of Jesus, you will stand before him confident and unashamed on the day he returns (1 John 2:28), and you can look forward to a time when there will ultimately be *no more shame* (Revelation 21:3–5).

But even now your nakedness and shame no longer define you. He has dressed you with clothing of salvation and draped you in a robe of righteousness (Isaiah 61:10). Jesus has covered your shame. You no longer bear the disgrace and identity of a slave. You are a daughter and an heir to the divine inheritance. Jesus enables you to be exposed in your weakness, to live naked and unashamed, because you know who you are and whose you are.

DESPAIR

When you despair, what is the lie you are choosing to believe? Your own sin, the sin of others, and the fallenness of this world often bring you to the end of yourself. Nothing is as you had dreamt or imagined; despair creeps in. Despair is the absence of hope. It springs from self-reliance and proud unbelief. Despair is shortsighted and is often accompanied by feelings of powerlessness and defeat.

A woman in despair is focused inward on self rather than outward on God. Never knowing she is denying the truth and hope of the life to come, she seeks to draw life and satisfaction from the things of this world, which leads to death—death of her hope and death of her faith.

When you live without eternity in view, you are tempted to seek your reward in this life. But when you are tossed about by the storms and circumstances of this life, you find yourself in despair. So you attempt to protect yourself from disappointment, or you attempt to draw life where none is to be found.

Hebrews 11 hails those who continued, in faith, to choose the truth of God over the lies of this world. In verses 13–16, the author recognizes "all these people died still believing what God had promised them. They did not receive what was promised, but they saw it all from a distance and welcomed it. They agreed that they were foreigners and nomads here on earth. Obviously, people who say such things are looking forward to a country they can call their own. If they had longed for the country they came from, they could have gone back. But they were looking for a better place, a heavenly homeland. That is why God is not ashamed to be called their God, for he has prepared a city for them" (Hebrews 11:13–16).

Like those children in Hebrews 11, you are a child of the promise. When you professed faith in Christ, you became a new creation. Your old life is gone, and a new life has begun (2 Corinthians 5:17–18). You have an entirely new potential, and your life is on a new trajectory—one that leads to a heavenly homeland. Because you have eternal life, you know that your years in this world are not where you will receive your final reward. You live looking forward to the heavenly city and the new life to come.

Questions for Reflection

1. What orphan tendencies do you most identify with (fear/control, guilt, shame, despair)? Why?

2. How do these tendencies hinder you in your calling as an essential counterpart?

3. What truths of the gospel do you need to believe in order to find freedom from your orphan tendencies (fear/control, shame, guilt, despair)?

LIVING LIKE A DAUGHTER

Only truth is an anchor for your soul. Only truth leads to life. The entire gospel is the announcement of truth that will free humanity from the lies we've believed since the garden. But what is that truth? Truth is a person; Jesus is the way, the truth, and the life (John 14:6). He came in the form of a man to set men and women free from their self-imposed slavery. Because of Jesus, Christians have the power of the Holy Spirit, who is the very Spirit of Truth (John 14:17). The Spirit lives within all believers, reminding them of and empowering them to live in truth.

As a daughter, your status is secure. You are holy and blameless already. You are counted as righteous already. You are free. You are a new creation in Christ.

But all of this is possible only because of Christ. Your identity is safe and secure because you are defined by who he is, not by who you are. "God is Redeemer; therefore, you are redeemed. God is Protector; therefore, you are safe. God is Ruler; therefore, you are under his control. God is Comforter; therefore, you are peaceful. God is Sustainer; therefore, you are hopeful. God is the One Who Sees; therefore, you are known and loved."[26]

How does a daughter live? *She lives as who she already is.*

> Dear friends, we are already God's children, but he has not yet shown us what we will be like when Christ appears. But

> we do know that we will be like him, for we will see him as he really is. And all who have this eager expectation will keep themselves pure, just as he is pure.
>
> —1 John 3:2–3

You do not have to live in self-protection. You can entrust yourself to him. You do not have to live in self-promotion. You can humble yourself before him, trusting that he will lift you up in honor in due time (1 Peter 5:6–7). You are free to be vulnerable and exposed.

You are free to be rejected. You are free to hold yourself out to another. You are free to invite, nurture, and partner because you are no longer self-focused and self-centered.

"What ultimately undoes the pull to self-protection is the cross. Jesus refused to seek the proof of his own protection because he was seeking more than his own protection. He was looking for you . . . You were outside the camp, cut off from the presence of God . . . Jesus didn't come to protect himself. He came for the world. He came for the church. He came for you. He bore your reproach, strapped on your curse, carried your exile. This other-directedness freed Jesus to live out a very different life from the cringing, anxiety-filled lives so many of us carry on."[27]

Jesus didn't shrink back in fear and self-protection. He was not concerned with himself. He knew all that would happen to him. He knew he would be rejected. He knew he would be mocked. He knew he would stand alone—naked and exposed for all to see. He knew, and he stepped forward (John 18:4). He stepped forward for you.

So how does a daughter live when her husband constantly rejects her? A daughter knows that even though Jesus was rejected by those he loved, he still held himself out to them as a source of life. A daughter knows that because of Christ, she is no longer rejected but chosen, adopted, loved, and accepted. Because she does not find her acceptance in her husband but in Christ, she is free to invite, nurture, and partner with him without fear of his rejection.

How does a daughter act when she's continually passed over for the promotion? How does she partner with her boss in spite of the fact that her boss continues to overlook her? A daughter knows that Jesus is King and reigns over all of her circumstances. She knows that he is trustworthy and good; she entrusts herself and her circumstances to him. A daughter does not rely on human recognition and reward. She does not need to build her own kingdom here because she is looking forward to the kingdom to come and knows her diligence will be rewarded then. This belief frees her to partner with her boss without expectation and resentment.

How does a daughter act in the face of injustice? A daughter knows and understands that God is just and holy. She knows that any injustice she faces will be righted. If the person who sinned against her is a believer, she knows that Jesus already paid the price for that sin, and justice has already been done. If the person who sinned against her is not a believer, she knows that the day of justice will come. Either way, she is free from a need to control or exact justice because she trusts in a God who is just and will repay and reward each according to what he has done (Jeremiah 17:10, Matthew 16:27, Romans 12:19).

How does a daughter who has unmet desires for children or marriage continue to live as an image-bearer in the face of her desires? A daughter trusts that God is for her and will provide her with all she needs for life and godliness. She is humble and understands that she does not know what is best for her. She knows that she may not love the season she is in, but she can trust and obey God in it. Because of this belief, she does not turn in on herself in despair and frustration; she continues to live with a posture of gratitude and humility.

How does a daughter who is worried about the safety and well-being of her children or their salvation continue to nurture and partner in ways that are encouraging and life giving? A daughter entrusts those she loves to God. She knows they are better in his hands than in hers. She is not ruled by fear or a need to control. She does not withdraw from them in self-protection, nor does she push her own agenda on them in self-promotion. She does not manipulate them to make a decision for her own comfort but challenges them and gives them room to think and grow. Ultimately, she rests in the God who created them and has determined their path before they were even born. Because she trusts God, she is able to move toward them, speaking truth and holding herself out to them as a source of life regardless of their responses.

Living as an orphan corrupts the image of God within you. But, if you are in Christ, you are not an orphan; you are a daughter. This is your story. Having been adopted into the family of God, you have been and are being redeemed; you are free. When you choose to believe this truth and all that encompasses it, you live in a way that reflects the glory of the image of God. You are free to invite, nurture, and partner.

But the irony of the gospel story is that you must lose your life to find it. You must surrender your rights to yourself and your search for happiness in order to find true joy. You must rest from your efforts to self-protect in order to find true peace and security. You must refrain from self-promoting to find the true contentment and worth you desire.

The gospel has already begun something new in you, *but* it is not yet completed in your character. It is a status that you already possess, but it is also a future reality that you are growing in. You were created with the capacity to invite, nurture, and partner. Sin fractured the image of God in you, but as a new creation, these attributes that were fallen are newly created, redeemed, resurrected. They are being restored, and they will continue to be restored until Jesus' return.

This present reality is fleeting and temporary. It is not a safe foundation upon which to build your life, hope, and identity. Rather, this life is shaping you and preparing you for future glory. But because we are so prone to forget, we must tell ourselves this gospel story over and over again. Daily choose to place yourself in the hands of the Master Storyteller, allowing him to craft and to create as he chooses. Entrust yourselves to him, remembering that he is for you, and he is committed to finishing the work he began in you (Philippians 1:6).

Questions for Reflection

1. Describe the freedom found in Christ. How does this free you from self-protection and self-promotion? How does it affect your ability to invite, nurture, and partner?

2. What does it mean to be a daughter? How does a daughter live?

3. Describe a situation in your life in which you lived like a daughter.

4. Describe a situation in your life in which you lived like an orphan. How might a daughter have responded differently?

5. In what way do you struggle to believe the truths of the gospel? In what way do you struggle to believe who you are in Christ? Why?

07

NOW WHAT?

EXPOSED

In the beginning, Adam and Eve lived in the garden—naked and unashamed. Their physical nakedness was also symbolic of their emotional and spiritual vulnerability. There was nothing hidden, nothing unknown to each other or to God. They enjoyed unhindered fellowship with one another and with God. That is, until they sinned.

> The woman was convinced. She saw that the tree was beautiful and its fruit looked delicious, and she wanted the wisdom it would give her. So she took some of the fruit and ate it. Then she gave some to her husband, who was with her, and he ate it too. At that moment their eyes were opened, and they suddenly felt shame at their nakedness. So they sewed fig leaves together to cover themselves. When the cool evening breezes were blowing, the man and his wife heard the Lord God walking about in the garden. So they hid from the Lord God among the trees. Then the Lord God called to the man, "Where are you?" He replied, "I heard you walking in the garden, so I hid. I was afraid because I was naked."
>
> —Genesis 3:6–10

After Adam and Eve sinned, their eyes were opened, they realized their nakedness, and they were ashamed. And so they sewed fig leaves together to cover their nakedness, to cover over their shame.

But more than Adam and Eve's bodies were exposed in the garden; their hearts were exposed as well. When they heard God walking in the garden, they hid. They hid from their Creator, their Father, the one who had abundantly provided for them. Rather than humbling themselves before him and confessing their offense, they covered themselves and hid in shame. Their once unhindered fellowship was broken.

Time and again, men and women's sinful deeds are exposed in Scripture: David's adultery and murder; Peter's denial of Jesus; and Ananias and Sapphira's deceit. While being exposed may be humbling, it does not have to be humiliating. Ananias and Sapphira did not repent when their sin was exposed; therefore they were humiliated, and it led to their deaths. David and Peter, however, humbled themselves and repented of their sin, and as a result, they were restored.

As you work through the last few chapters, you may feel exposed in your sin of autonomy, or self-protection and self-promotion. Maybe you feel frustrated in your failure to invite, nurture, and partner well. Maybe you are wrestling with what you are supposed to do now. To be certain, exposure, being known in your sin and weakness, is part of the Christian life. It is important to be active in the battle against sin, shedding light on the indwelling sin within you.

> For once you were full of darkness, but now you have light from the Lord. So live as people of light! For this light within you produces only what is good and right and true. Carefully determine what pleases the Lord. Take no part in the worthless deeds of evil and darkness; instead, expose them. It is shameful even to talk about the things that ungodly people do in secret. But their evil intentions will be exposed when the light shines on them, for the light makes everything visible.
>
> —Ephesians 5:8–14a

Move toward others and allow them to know you in your struggles, failings, and weaknesses. Placing yourself in authentic, honest relationships is crucial to growing in Christian maturity. As the Holy Spirit sheds light on your sin, resist the temptation to hide and cover, or appear as if you have it all together. This is harmful not only to you but also to others.

Allowing others to know you in your weakness helps them understand more fully what it means to be a Christian. Being a Christian does not mean you have it all together or that you never sin. On the contrary, being a Christian means that you recognize your sinful nature apart from Christ, and that you believe Christ's life, death, and resurrection is your only hope.

Questions for Reflection

1. Do you have a Christian community with whom you can be transparent? If not, what steps do you need to take to become part of such a group?

2. Where is God calling you to biblical community? How do you need to respond?

3. If you are part of a group that does not have this level of transparency, how can you change that?

REPENTANCE

WORLDLY SORROW VERSUS GODLY SORROW

Knowing who God created you to be as a woman does not mean you can live perfectly. On this side of heaven, sin will continue to be a very real battle. It is one thing to know you are sinner or to recognize the ways in which you are sinful. It is quite another thing, however, to respond in a godly way. David knew this well, and it is reflected in his response to the Lord after his adulterous affair with Bathsheba was exposed.

> You do not desire a sacrifice, or I would offer one.
>
> You do not want a burnt offering.
>
> The sacrifice you desire is a broken spirit.
>
> You will not reject a broken and repentant heart, O God.
>
> —Psalm 51:16–17

A guilty conscience does not necessarily mean you are repentant. Often, the feeling of guilt is rooted in proud unbelief. You think that you should know better, be better, or do better, and so you try harder to manage your sin and to earn God's favor. But this is not living in light of the gospel. It is, instead, just a modern-day version of sacrifices and burnt offerings. This is not the heart of repentance; it is penance—working to gain God's forgiveness through behavior modification. This type of sorrow leads to slavery and death, not freedom, because you can never do enough to be worthy.

Likewise, sorrowful, tear-filled confessions do not necessarily mean you are repentant either. Repentance based solely on human emotion is self-centered and self-pitying, rooted in the belief that if you feel bad enough and cry long enough, you will prove you are worthy of forgiveness. This type of sorrow also leads to despair and slavery because you can never be sorry enough to earn God's forgiveness.

In 2 Corinthians 7:10, Paul describes two types of sorrow over sin: worldly sorrow and godly sorrow.

> For the kind of sorrow God wants us to experience leads us away from sin and results in salvation. There's no regret for that kind of sorrow. But worldly sorrow, which lacks repentance, results in spiritual death.
>
> —2 Corinthians 7:10

As the Spirit convicts, you may have trouble determining whether what you are feeling is godly or worldly sorrow. Paul says you can identify these sorrows by the fruit they produce. Godly sorrow leads to salvation, life, and freedom. Worldly sorrow leads to death, despair, and slavery.

This is evident in the life of Paul. As one who persecuted the early church and oversaw the murders and imprisonment of many of Jesus' followers, Paul had every reason to feel worldly sorrow and unrelenting shame over his past sin. But Paul knew he was not just a sinner *before* believing in Jesus. Even at the end of his ministry, in a letter to Timothy, Paul called himself *chief of sinners.* He was a man who knew the depth of his sinfulness.

> And I know that nothing good lives in me, that is, in my sinful nature. I want to do what is right, but I can't. I want to do what is good, but I don't. I don't want to do what is wrong, but I do it anyway. But if I do what I don't want to do, I am not really the one doing wrong; it is sin living in me that does it. I have discovered this principle of life—that when I want to do what is right, I inevitably do what is wrong. I love God's law with all my heart. But there is another power within me that is at war with my mind. This power makes me a slave to the sin that is still within me. Oh, what a miserable person I am! Who

> will free me from this life that is dominated by sin and death? Thank God! The answer is in Jesus Christ our Lord.
>
> —Romans 7:18–25a

Paul understood a believer's battle with sin, and while he does lament over his sin in this passage, these are not the words of a man experiencing worldly sorrow. He knew and humbly proclaimed his own wretchedness, but he did not lament as one who had no hope. Paul knew the answer to his sin problem: "Oh, what a miserable person I am! Who will free me from this life that is dominated by sin and death? Thank God! The answer is in Jesus Christ our Lord."

True repentance isn't self-focused; it is God-focused, and it leads to life. Again, this is evident in Paul's life. Immediately following Paul's discourse on sin in the above passage, he launches into what is possibly one of the most beautiful, poignant passages in the New Testament:

> So now there is no condemnation for those who belong to Christ Jesus. And because you belong to him, the power of the life-giving Spirit has freed you from the power of sin that leads to death . . . And Christ lives within you, so even though your body will die because of sin, the Spirit gives you life because you have been made right with God . . . And we know that God causes everything to work together for the good of those who love God and are called according to his purpose for them. For God knew his people in advance, and he chose them to become like his Son, so that his Son would be the firstborn among many brothers and sisters. And having chosen them, he called them to come to him. And having called them, he gave them right standing with himself. And having given them right standing, he gave them his glory. What shall we say about such wonderful things as these? If God is for us, who can ever be against us? Since he did not spare even his own Son but gave him up for us all, won't he also give us everything else? Who dares accuse us whom God

> has chosen for his own? No one—for God himself has given us right standing with himself. Who then will condemn us? No one—for Christ Jesus died for us and was raised to life for us, and he is sitting in the place of honor at God's right hand, pleading for us. Can anything ever separate us from Christ's love? Does it mean he no longer loves us if we have trouble or calamity, or are persecuted, or hungry, or destitute, or in danger, or threatened with death? (As the Scriptures say, "For your sake we are killed every day; we are being slaughtered like sheep.") No, despite all these things, overwhelming victory is ours through Christ, who loved us. And I am convinced that nothing can ever separate us from God's love. Neither death nor life, neither angels nor demons, neither our fears for today nor our worries about tomorrow—not even the powers of hell can separate us from God's love. No power in the sky above or in the earth below—indeed, nothing in all creation will ever be able to separate us from the love of God that is revealed in Christ Jesus our Lord.
>
> —Romans 8:1–2, 10, 28–39

These are not the words of a man who felt like a victim of his sin. Paul did not believe he was defined by his sin, failure, or weakness. Paul's focus was on God's glory. Rather than being mired in grief and despair over his sin, he rejoiced in God's great mercy. Paul knew that true repentance meant not only turning *from* his sin, but also turning *to* Jesus Christ. He was humbled by his sin, but he was also freed and emboldened by the gospel.

Paul knew and believed the gospel. It had pierced his soul and settled into the marrow of his bones. It was the wellspring of his life; it was the source of his strength and the passion of his existence. Paul was transformed by the glory, mercy, compassion, faithfulness, and grace of God in the face of Jesus Christ. And it was from this understanding that he was able to declare himself the chief of sinners.

It was not a false humility or a self-abasement. He did not live chained to his sin, nor did he hide in shame. On the contrary, knowing the depth of his sinfulness freed him. He boldly and humbly declared himself a sinner who rested solely on the good news of Jesus Christ as payment for his sins. Paul knew salvation had nothing to do with his observance of the law, his pedigree, his knowledge, or his successful ministry. He knew he was a sinner in need of a Savior.

True repentance means movement—movement away from sin and toward Christ. It begins with a change of mind that leads to a change of direction, then to a change of heart, and finally to a changed life.[28] Take, for example, a woman who has been engaged in sex outside of marriage. True repentance begins with a change of mind, acknowledging that her actions are sinful and offensive to God, and then choosing to believe in his truth. Her next step would be to change direction by ending her sexual relationships and moving into biblical community to work through her struggle. As a result of this change in mind and direction, her heart begins to change, and the result is a transformed life.

The repentance process may take days, months, or years. At times, it will be painful, and it will require you to do difficult things. But as you continue to move toward God and others, the result is a life free of the bondage of shame and guilt.

Questions for Reflection

1. What actions do you need to take to express true repentance? What's holding you back?

2. Where is God working to change your heart and transform your life?

THE SAMARITAN WOMAN

REPENTANCE UNTO LIFE

It was the heat of the day when she went to draw water from the well. Most women drew their water in the cool of the morning or evening, but in the middle of the day, she was less likely to run into anyone. When she arrived at the well, she found a Jewish man sitting there. This was highly unusual. Most Jews would travel a great distance to avoid Samaria. She was even more surprised when he spoke to her and asked her for a drink from her water jar.

Samaritans were a people of mixed Jewish and Gentile heritage. Both Jew and Gentile looked down on the Samaritans, viewing them as a ceremonially unclean people. By merely associating with her, he could be considered unclean. But that didn't stop him. He continued to engage her in conversation about water, living water. She didn't understand what he was talking about. How could the water he had to offer be better than that of her ancestors who had built the well? But he seemed insistent that the water he offered her would satisfy her thirst forever.

She liked the thought that she might never have to go to the well to draw water again, but when she asked him for this water, he told her to go get her husband. He had just uncovered her shame—she had no husband, though she was living with a man. When she told him she didn't have a husband,

> he told her he already knew she didn't! As a matter of fact, he knew all about her. He knew she'd had five husbands and that the man she lived with now wasn't her husband.
>
> How did he know all of that? He must be a prophet. Maybe he could tell her why the Jews and Samaritans were divided over where they should worship. Instead of answering her question, all he did was tell her that a time was coming when they would worship in neither place. She would just have to wait for the long-awaited Messiah; he would answer her question. But then, the conversation took another unexpected turn when Jesus told her, "I AM the Messiah."
>
> —John 4:7–26 (paraphrase)

Based on historical context and the available details of the Samaritan woman's life, it is reasonable to discern that this woman was likely an outcast of outcasts, isolated from those within her own community. Her life choices and her circumstances drove her to draw water alone in the heat of the day, while most women did so in the cool of the morning or evening.

Jesus met this woman in her sin and isolation and refused to allow her to hide. He was not afraid of being considered ceremonially unclean, nor was he concerned with the ramifications of engaging her. On the contrary, he initiated their conversation, exposing her sin and uncovering the source of her shame—she had been married five times, and the man she was living with wasn't her husband.

It is unclear whether her previous husbands died or divorced her. Regardless of the reason, for a woman living in this time, to have been married five times carried great shame. Jesus' encounter with this woman is remarkable in so many ways. He was not only a man associating one-on-one with a woman but also a Jew who was associating with a Samaritan. To make matters worse, this Samaritan woman was not even in good standing within her own community. And yet it was to this very woman that Jesus chose to reveal his identity as the Messiah.

When the Samaritan woman encountered Jesus, she was freed from her shame. So much so that she ran to tell the same people she had been running from. Many Samaritans believed in Jesus because of this woman's testimony (John 4:39). Being known by Jesus so transformed her that others believed her message, in spite of the fact that she was an unlikely messenger.

She found freedom in being truly, intimately known. Jesus knew everything about her—everything she had done, all the bad choices, all the moral failures. Instead of being demoralized by this, she found a new freedom, a new identity, a new hope. She was no longer subject to hiding and avoidance but instead boldly proclaimed the joys of being fully known.

Interestingly, this story marks the first indication that Jesus came to bring salvation to the whole world, not just the Jews. When she was exposed, this woman was led to godly repentance, which led to life, freedom, restoration, joy, worship, and ultimately the advancement of the kingdom.

Just as Jesus dealt with the Samaritan woman, he will deal with you. He will not allow you to hide. The Spirit exposes and convicts but not to bring guilt, shame, and despair. The Spirit convicts to bring life. When Jesus exposes your sin and you respond in godly sorrow, the result is freedom, joy, and restoration.

Remarkably, it doesn't end with you. Jesus takes the very source of your deepest shame and uses it in a way that draws others to himself. He is so great and merciful a Savior that he will not allow even your sin to go to waste. By allowing yourself to be known, you will witness the redeeming grace of God as he uses your source of shame in a way that brings him glory and expands his kingdom. He can and will do it if you allow him.

Questions for Reflection

1. What is your deepest source of shame?

2. How might God use that to bring glory to himself and others to relationship with him?

3. Are you willing to be exposed in your shame to experience the freedom, restoration, and joy that only Jesus can bring?

NOTES

1. Flinn, Hilary. "What Does It Mean To Be A Woman Today?" *My Cravings Blog,* August 13, 2015. Retrieved from http://mycravings.ca/what-does-it-mean-to-be-a-woman-today/.

2. Rothschild, Nathalie. "A Country Tries to Banish Gender." *Slate Magazine,* April 11, 2012. Retrieved from https://slate.com/human-interest/2012/04/hen-swedens-new-gender-neutral-pronoun-causes-controversy.html.

3. Duke, Alan. "Miss Universe Pageant Ends Ban on Transgender Contestants." CNN, April 10, 2012. Retrieved from http://www.cnn.com/2012/04/10/ showbiz/miss-universe-transgender/index.html.

4. Bolick, Kate. "All the Single Ladies." *The Atlantic Magazine,* November, 2011. Retrieved from http://www.theatlantic.com/magazine/ archive/2011/11/all-the-single-ladies/8654/1/.

5. Mayo Clinic Staff. "Depression in Women: Understanding the Gender Gap." *Mayo Clinic,* 2010. Retrieved from http://www.mayoclinic.com/ health/depression/MH00035.

6. Keller, Tim. "The Centrality of the Gospel." 2001. Retrieved from http:// download.redeemer.com/pdf/learn/resources/Centrality_of_the_Gospel- Keller.pdf.

7. Smith, Claire. "The Original Man and Woman: Genesis 1–3." In *God's Good Design: What the Bible Really Says about Men and Women,* 180. Kingsford, N.S.W.: Matthias Media, 2008.

8. Blanchard, Ken, P. Hodges, L. Ross, A. Willis. "Week Two." *Lead Like Jesus,* 30. Nashville, Tenn.: Thomas Nelson Book Group, 2003.

9. Lloyd-Jones, Sally. "The Story and the Song." In *Jesus Storybook Bible,* 12. Grand Rapids, Michigan: Zondervan, 2007.

10. Piper, John. "Group Study Guide" In *Desiring God,* 313. Colorado Springs, Colorado: Multnomah Books, 1987.

11. Lewis, C. S. "The Great Divorce." *The Complete C.S. Lewis Signature Classics,* 528–29. San Francisco, Calif.: Harper San Francisco, 2002.

12. Henry, Matthew. "Luke 2." *Matthew Henry Commentary,* 1706. Bible Study Tools. Retrieved from http://www.biblestudytools.com/commentaries/matthew-henry-concise.html.

13. *Merriam-Webster.* An Encyclopædia Britannica Company. Retrieved from http://www.merriam-webster.com/dictionary/nurture.

14. Moore, Russell D. "Free Falling." *Tempted and Tried,* 115. Wheaton, Illinois: Crossway Books, 2011.

15. Tripp, Paul D. "Establishing Agenda and Clarifying Responsibility." *Instruments in the Redeemer's Hands,* 250. Phillipsburg, New Jersey: P&R Publishing, 2002.

16. Ibid, 254.

17. "Bible Notes." *ESV Study Bible,* 2007. Wheaton, Illinois: Crossway Bibles, 2008.

18. Moore, *Tempted and Tried,* 116.

19. "Bible Notes." *ESV Study Bible,* 2179.

20. Keller, "Centrality of the Gospel."

21. Ibid.

22. Henry, "Matthew 11."

23. Ibid.

24. Bridges, Jerry. "The Scapegoat." *The Gospel for Real Life,* 62. Colorado Springs, Colorado: NavPress, 2002.

25. Brown, B. (2010, June). Brene Brown: The Power of Vulnerability [Video file]. Retrieved from http://www.ted.com/talks/brene_brown_on_vulnerability.html.

26. Delk, Ruthie. "Living as His Child." *Craving Grace Like Chocolate,* 52–53. CreateSpace Independent Publishing, 2012.

27. Moore, *Tempted and Tried,* 113.

28. Driscoll, Mark. "Comfort Over Christ?" *Pastor Mark Driscoll Blog,* June 19, 2012. Retrieved from http://markdriscoll.org/sermons/lukewarm-in-lacodicea-comfort-and-convenience-before-christ/

APPENDIX 1

SCRIPTURE REFERENCES

All too often we listen to lies instead of intentionally preaching the truth of the gospel to ourselves. The following verse references are helpful to memorize and call to mind when battling thoughts and feelings of fear, guilt, shame, and despair.

GUILT TO DECLARED NOT GUILTY

Romans 3:10–12: As the Scriptures say, no one is righteous—not even one. No one is truly wise; no one is seeking God. All have turned away; all have become useless. No one does good, not a single one.

Romans 3:23–26: For everyone has sinned; we all fall short of God's glorious standard. Yet God, with undeserved kindness, declares that we are righteous. He did this through Christ Jesus when he freed us from the penalty for our sins. For God presented Jesus as the sacrifice for sin. People are made right with God when they believe that Jesus sacrificed his life, shedding his blood. This sacrifice shows that God was being fair when he held back and did not punish those who sinned in times past, for he was looking ahead and including them in what he would do in this present time. God did this to demonstrate his righteousness, for he himself is fair and just, and he declares sinners to be right in his sight when they believe in Jesus.

Romans 5:8–9: But God showed his great love for us by sending Christ to die for us while we were still sinners. And since we have been made right in God's sight by the blood of Christ, he will certainly save us from God's condemnation.

Romans 5:17–19: For the sin of this one man, Adam, caused death to rule over many. But even greater is God's wonderful grace and his gift

of righteousness, for all who receive it will live in triumph over sin and death through this one man, Jesus Christ. Yes, Adam's one sin brings condemnation for everyone, but Christ's one act of righteousness brings a right relationship with God and new life for everyone. Because one person disobeyed God, many became sinners. But because one other person obeyed God, many will be made righteous.

Romans 8:1–2: So now there is no condemnation for those who belong to Christ Jesus. And because you belong to him, the power of the life-giving Spirit has freed you from the power of sin that leads to death.

2 Corinthians 5:19–21: For God was in Christ, reconciling the world to himself, no longer counting people's sins against them. And he gave us this wonderful message of reconciliation. So we are Christ's ambassadors; God is making his appeal through us. We speak for Christ when we plead, "Come back to God!"

Galatians 2:16: Yet we know that a person is made right with God by faith in Jesus Christ, not by obeying the law. And we have believed in Christ Jesus, so that we might be made right with God because of our faith in Christ, not because we have obeyed the law. For no one will ever be made right with God by obeying the law.

Galatians 3:11–14: So it is clear that no one can be made right with God by trying to keep the law. For the Scriptures say, "It is through faith that a righteous person has life." This way of faith is very different from the way of law, which says, "It is through obeying the law that a person has life." But Christ has rescued us from the curse pronounced by the law. When he was hung on the cross, he took upon himself the curse for our wrongdoing. For it is written in the Scriptures, "Cursed is everyone who is hung on a tree." Through Christ Jesus, God has blessed the Gentiles with the same blessing he promised to Abraham, so that we who are believers might receive the promised Holy Spirit through faith.

Philippians 3:8–10: Yes, everything else is worthless when compared with the infinite value of knowing Christ Jesus my Lord. For his sake I have discarded everything else, counting it all as garbage, so that I could gain Christ and become one with him. I no longer count on my own righteousness through obeying the law; rather, I become righteous through faith in Christ. For God's way of making us right with himself depends on faith. I want to know Christ and experience the mighty power that raised him from the dead. I want to suffer with him, sharing in his death.

Colossians 2:13–14: You were dead because of your sins and because your sinful nature was not yet cut away. Then God made you alive with Christ, for he forgave all our sins. He canceled the record of the charges against us and took it away by nailing it to the cross.

Hebrews 10:11–17: Under the old covenant, the priest stands and ministers before the altar day after day, offering the same sacrifices again and again, which can never take away sins. But our High Priest offered himself to God as a single sacrifice for sins, good for all time. Then he sat down in the place of honor at God's right hand. There he waits until his enemies are humbled and made a footstool under his feet. For by that one offering he forever made perfect those who are being made holy. And the Holy Spirit also testifies that this is so. For he says, "This is the new covenant I will make with my people on that day, says the LORD: I will put my laws in their hearts, and I will write them on their minds." Then he says, I will never again remember their sins and lawless deeds."

SHAME TO ADOPTION

Romans 8:14–17: For all who are led by the Spirit of God are children of God. So you have not received a spirit that makes you fearful slaves. Instead, you received God's Spirit when he adopted you as his own children. Now we call him, "Abba, Father." For his Spirit joins with our spirit to affirm that we are God's children. And since we are his children, we are his heirs. In fact, together with Christ we are heirs of God's glory. But if we are to share his glory, we must also share his suffering.

Galatians 4:4–7: But when the right time came, God sent his Son, born of a woman, subject to the law. God sent him to buy freedom for us who were slaves to the law, so that he could adopt us as his very own children And because we are his children, God has sent the Spirit of his Son into our hearts, prompting us to call out, "Abba, Father." Now you are no longer a slave but God's own child. And since you are his child, God has made you his heir.

Ephesians 1:5–8: God decided in advance to adopt us into his own family by bringing us to himself through Jesus Christ. This is what he wanted to do, and it gave him great pleasure. So we praise God for the glorious grace he has poured out on us who belong to his dear Son. He is so rich in kindness and grace that he purchased our freedom with the blood of his Son and forgave our sins. He has showered his kindness on us, along with all wisdom and understanding.

1 John 3:1–2: See how very much our Father loves us, for he calls us his children, and that is what we are! But the people who belong to this world don't recognize that we are God's children because they don't know him. Dear friends, we are already God's children, but he has not yet shown us what we will be like when Christ appears. But we do know that we will be like him, for we will see him as he really is.

FEAR TO HOPE

Romans 5:1–2: Therefore, since we have been made right in God's sight by faith, we have peace with God because of what Jesus Christ our Lord has done for us. Because of our faith, Christ has brought us into this place of undeserved privilege where we now stand, and we confidently and joyfully look forward to sharing God's glory.

Ephesians 1:18–20: I pray that your hearts will be flooded with light so that you can understand the confident hope he has given to those he called—his holy people who are his rich and glorious inheritance. I also pray that you will understand the incredible greatness of God's power for us who believe him. This is the same mighty power that raised Christ from the dead and seated him in the place of honor at God's right hand in the heavenly realms.

Philippians 3:13–14: No, dear brothers and sisters, I have not achieved it, but I focus on this one thing: Forgetting the past and looking forward to what lies ahead, I press on to reach the end of the race and receive the heavenly prize for which God, through Christ Jesus, is calling us.

Philippians 3:20–21: But we are citizens of heaven, where the Lord Jesus Christ lives. And we are eagerly waiting for him to return as our Savior. He will take our weak mortal bodies and change them into glorious bodies like his own, using the same power with which he will bring everything under his control.

Hebrews 6:17–20: God also bound himself with an oath, so that those who received the promise could be perfectly sure that he would never change his mind. So God has given both his promise and his oath. These two things are unchangeable because it is impossible for God to lie. Therefore, we who have fled to him for refuge can have great confidence as we hold to the hope that lies before us. This hope is a strong and trustworthy anchor for our souls. It leads us through the curtain into God's inner sanctuary. Jesus has already gone in there for us. He has become our eternal High Priest in the order of Melchizedek.

Hebrews 10:21–24: And since we have a great High Priest who rules over God's house, let us go right into the presence of God with sincere hearts fully trusting him. For our guilty consciences have been sprinkled with Christ's blood to make us clean, and our bodies have been washed with pure water. Let us hold tightly without wavering to the hope we affirm, for God can be trusted to keep his promise. Let us think of ways to motivate one another to acts of love and good works.

1 Peter 1:3–5: All praise to God, the Father of our Lord Jesus Christ. It is by his great mercy that we have been born again, because God raised Jesus Christ from the dead. Now we live with great expectation, and we have a priceless inheritance—an inheritance that is kept in heaven for you, pure and undefiled, beyond the reach of change and decay. And through your faith, God is protecting you by his power until you receive this salvation, which is ready to be revealed on the last day for all to see.

1 John 4:18–19: Such love has no fear, because perfect love expels all fear. If we are afraid, it is for fear of punishment, and this shows that we have not fully experienced his perfect love. We love each other because he loved us first.

DESPAIR (POWERLESSNESS) TO NEW BIRTH

John 1:12–13: But to all who believed him and accepted him, he gave the right to become children of God. They are reborn—not with a physical birth resulting from human passion or plan, but a birth that comes from God.

John 3:3–8: Jesus replied, "I tell you the truth, unless you are born again, you cannot see the kingdom of God." "What do you mean?" exclaimed Nicodemus. "How can an old man go back into his mother's womb and be born again?" Jesus replied, "I assure you, no one can enter the kingdom of God without being born of water and the Spirit. Humans can reproduce only human life, but the Holy Spirit gives birth to spiritual life. So don't be surprised when I say, 'You must be born again.' The wind blows wherever it wants. Just as you can hear the wind but can't tell where it comes from or where it is going, so you can't explain how people are born of the Spirit."

Romans 6:4–5: For we died and were buried with Christ by baptism. And just as Christ was raised from the dead by the glorious power of the Father, now we also may live new lives. Since we have been united with him in his death, we will also be raised to life as he was.

2 Corinthians 5:17–18: This means that anyone who belongs to Christ has become a new person. The old life is gone; a new life has begun! And all of this is a gift from God, who brought us back to himself through Christ. And God has given us this task of reconciling people to him.

2 Corinthians 9:8: And God will generously provide all you need. Then you will always have everything you need and plenty left over to share with others.

2 Corinthians 12:9–10: Each time he said, "My grace is all you need. My power works best in weakness." So now I am glad to boast about my weaknesses, so that the power of Christ can work through me. That's why I take pleasure in my weaknesses and in the insults, hardships, persecutions, and troubles that I suffer for Christ. For when I am weak, then I am strong.

Galatians 3:26: For you are all children of God through faith in Christ Jesus.

Ephesians 2:4–6: But God is so rich in mercy, and he loved us so much, that even though we were dead because of our sins, he gave us life when he raised Christ from the dead. (It is only by God's grace that you have been saved!) For he raised us from the dead along with Christ and seated us with him in the heavenly realms because we are united with Christ Jesus.

SLAVERY TO FREEDOM

John 8:31–36: Jesus said to the people who believed in him, "You are truly my disciples if you remain faithful to my teachings. And you will know the truth, and the truth will set you free." "But we are descendants of Abraham," they said. "We have never been slaves to anyone. What do you mean, 'You will be set free'?" Jesus replied, "I tell you the truth, everyone who sins is a slave of sin. A slave is not a permanent member of the family, but a son is part of the family forever. So if the Son sets you free, you are truly free."

Romans 8:15–17: So you have not received a spirit that makes you fearful slaves. Instead, you received God's Spirit when he adopted you as his own children. Now we call him, "Abba, Father." For his Spirit joins with our spirit to affirm that we are God's children. And since we are his children, we are his heirs. In fact, together with Christ we are heirs of God's glory. But if we are to share his glory, we must also share his suffering.

2 Corinthians 3:17–18: For the Lord is the Spirit, and wherever the Spirit of the Lord is, there is freedom. So all of us who have had that veil removed can see and reflect the glory of the Lord. And the Lord—who is the Spirit—makes us more and more like him as we are changed into his glorious image.

Galatians 5:1, 13: So Christ has truly set us free. Now make sure that you stay free, and don't get tied up again in slavery to the law . . . For you have been called to live in freedom, my brothers and sisters. But don't use your freedom to satisfy your sinful nature. Instead, use your freedom to serve one another in love.

Hebrews 2:14–15: Because God's children are human beings—made of flesh and blood—the Son also became flesh and blood. For only as a human being could he die, and only by dying could he break the power of the devil, who had the power of death. Only in this way could he set free all who have lived their lives as slaves to the fear of dying.

APPENDIX 2

A GENTLE AND QUIET SPIRIT

- Is rooted confidently in God's goodness
- Has a correct view of God—who he is and who I am not
- Is settled and at peace with God's directions, plans, uncertainties, and mysteriousness
- Has an abiding trust in God's goodness and eager expectancy of his unpredictability
- Is unshakeable by circumstance (good or bad; not easily "puffed up" or "deflated")
- Is steady and resolute in convictions
- Is comfortable with a lack of control
- Is perceptive of and sensitive to others' perspectives; no felt need to impose one's own experience or paradigm on others
- Is genuinely accepting of others as they are, without condoning or enabling destructive thoughts and behaviors
- Is more concerned with the needs of others than protecting self
- Lives without regrets, confident that God can redeem all things—yet graciously accepting of consequences
- Is in constant ongoing conversation with God—the good, bad, and ugly
- Embraces one's own "humanness"/limits
- Is comfortable that life "isn't fair" and that God does not work systematically or in patterns

- Holds a bottom-line belief in and gratitude for God's mercy and grace, even and especially when nothing else is going "according to plan"
- Has a disposition and posture of deep gratitude, regardless of circumstance
- Has a spirit enlivened, nourished, and led by his Spirit
- Is "keeping in step with the Spirit" (Galatians 5)
- Is confident in how God created me (physically, emotionally, cognitively, psychologically, etc.) and who he created me to be and to reflect
- Is aware that I don't know what is truly good or best for me/others—abandonment of self-reliance
- Is self-accepting
- Is stable
- Has an inner core of satisfaction
- Accepts one's physical and mental realities as God-given
- Feels no need to defend or "prove" oneself
- Is not easily disturbed or offended
- Sees herself as broken, therefore is gentle with the faults of others
- Understands what is really important and what is not
- Takes the "long view," especially in conflict
- Is patient with others and herself
- Laughs a lot, especially at herself
- Lives in freedom from always needing to be right or competent
- Is very accepting and non-judgmental—draws others to herself

- Is "centered"
- Trusts God to change circumstances if/when it pleases him, or to change one's own heart
- Is not self-protective or suspicious of being taken advantage of
- Is generous with time and resources
- Has the ability and desire to make others comfortable
- Is teachable, always open to learn and change
- Is a safe place to come or "land"
- Has a "faith vision" of others, believing the best and, if disappointed, is gracious
- Does not cower or shy away from suffering, grief, or conflict
- Sees life as an adventure
- Hopes in the certainty of things to come (enables/adds to the "long view")
- Is content in the here and now, regardless of circumstance—by maintaining sight of the best that is yet to come and Who is preparing it
- Genuinely enjoys God
- Does not try to "box God in," categorize him, or explain him
- Lives joyfully in mystery
- Does the "next thing"
- Makes the mental/attitude adjustment
- Doesn't blame others/accuse/deflect
- Quickly forgives, including self
- Leaves oneself alone—does not obsess over self (image, intellect, etc.)
- Is free from others' opinions

- Is free from the tyranny of the urgent
- Does not lie to oneself—"you desire truth in my inmost being"
- Lives "unhurried"
- Is willing to embrace and enjoy life's detours—looks for God's redemptive hand in everything
- Is willing to give every cherished "possession" back to him (family members, relationships, jobs, things, etc.)—open-handedness, holds things loosely
- Refuses to be petty/catty
- Controls the tongue, knows when not to speak
- Desires and pursues an organic, growing relationship with God, and consequently others

For more information about

Biblical Femininity please visit:

grace.sc/ezer

info@grace.sc

Biblical Femininity is an Ezer resource from Grace Church.

The Ezer ministry exists to help women "throw off everything that hinders and the sin that so easily entangles" so that they may run the race with perseverance (Hebrews 12:1b). We desire to disciple women by providing accessible and practical biblically-based material that helps women find freedom from sin and brokenness and move toward spiritual maturity in Christ.

Also by Chrystie Cole and Grace Church

Redeeming Sexuality: Inviting God to Mend Our Fractured Hearts

Body Matters: A Biblical Understanding of the Body and Why it Matters in an Age of Discontent

A Woman's Words: Getting to the Heart of Our Speech

Shame: Finding Freedom

Seven Arrows: Studying Philippians Together
**method created by Matt Rogers*

All available through Grace Church | grace.sc

For our additional resources like our video-based study, Shame: Finding Freedom, the Stewarding Strength Journal, or to subscribe to the Ezer Equipped Newsletter please visit:

grace.sc/ezer

Our corresponding studies for men are

Authentic Manhood

Quest for Purity

A Man and His Wife

Sons and Daughters

A Man and His Work

Made in the USA
Columbia, SC
16 February 2024